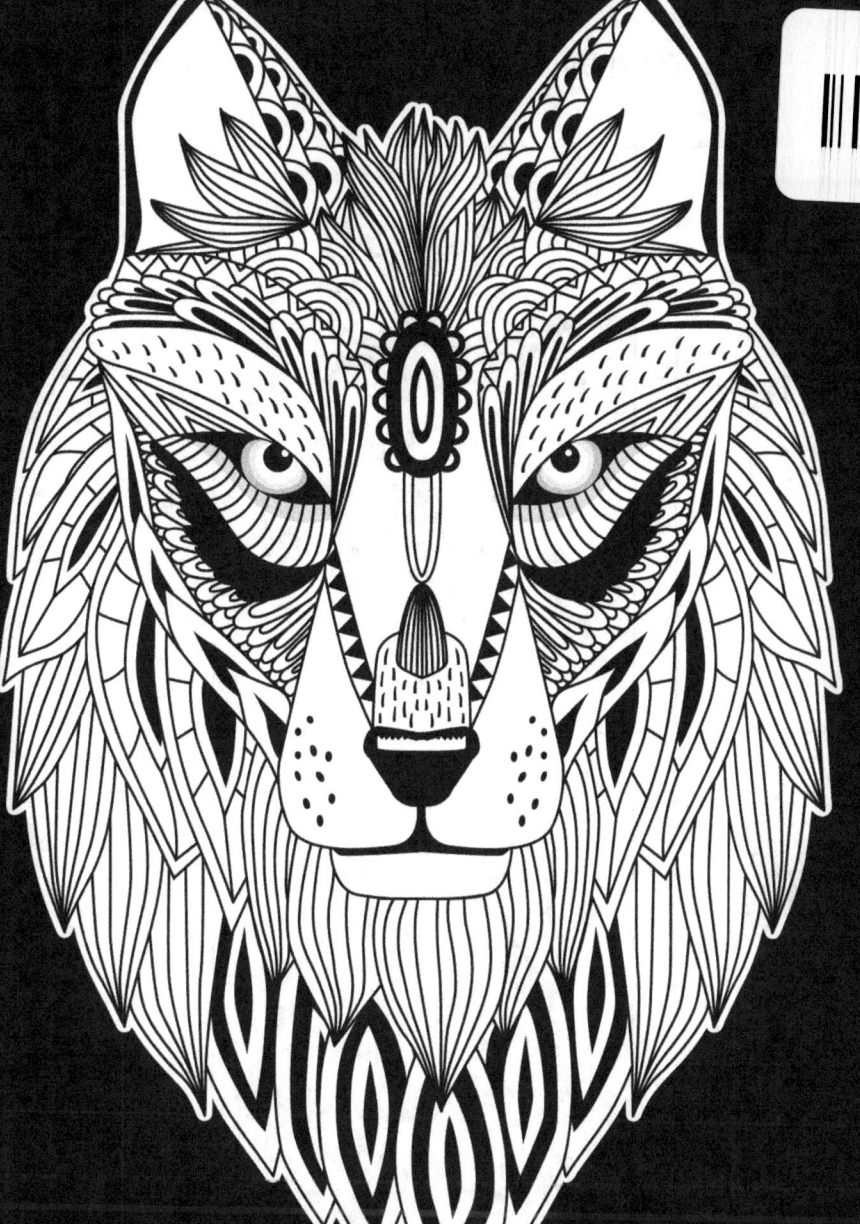

WOLF
COLORING BOOK
FOR ADULTS

▲ ART THERAPY COLORING

Preview of Coloring Pages

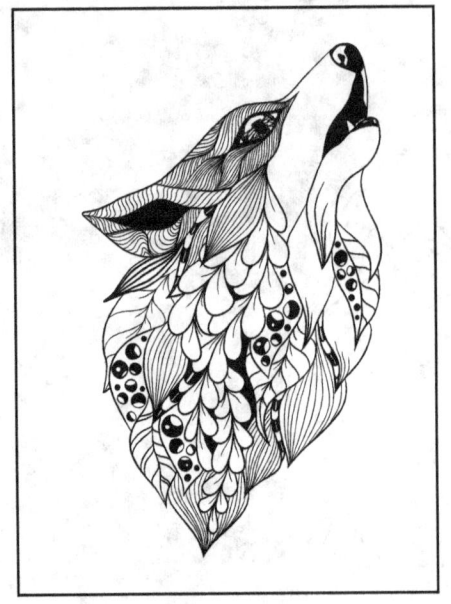
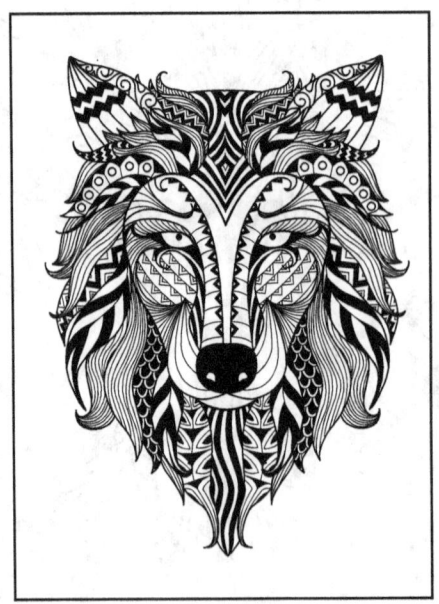
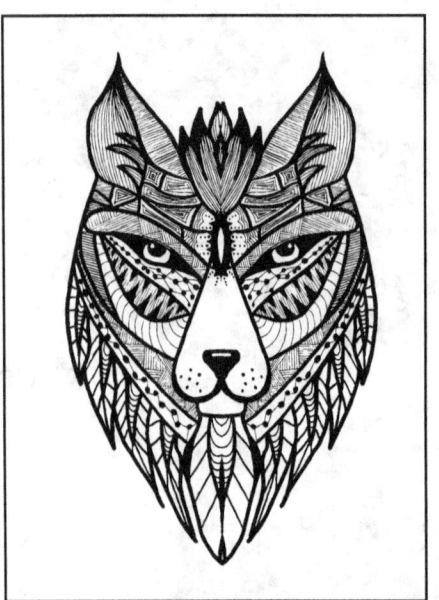
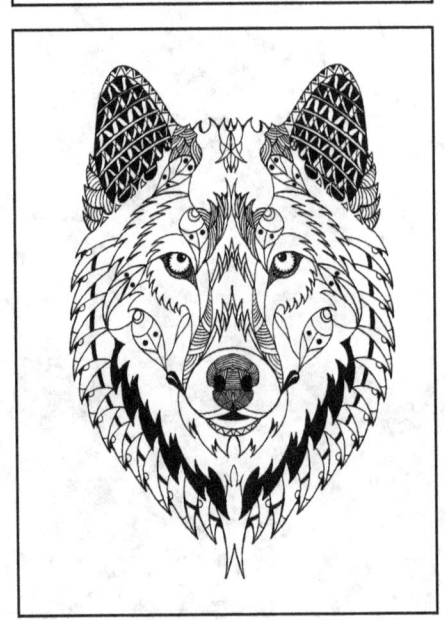
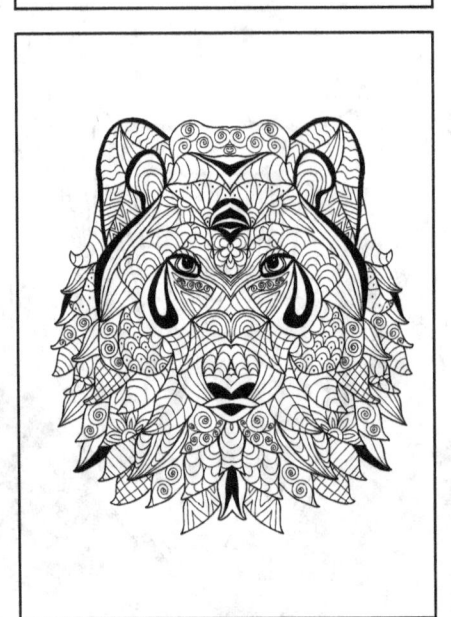
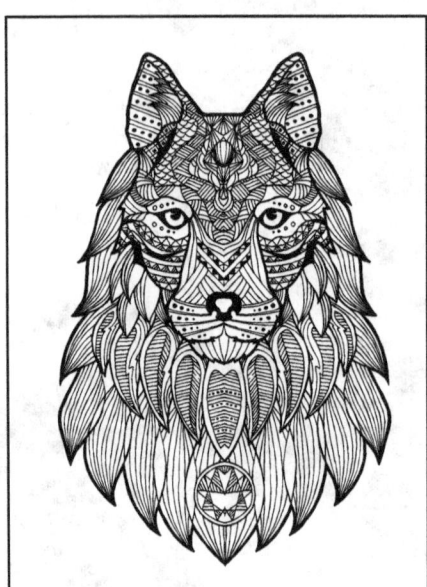
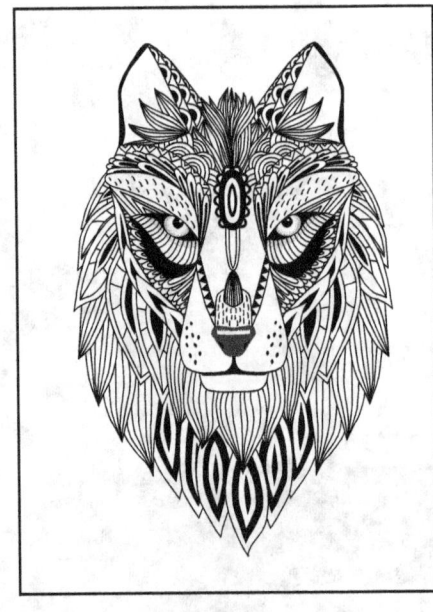
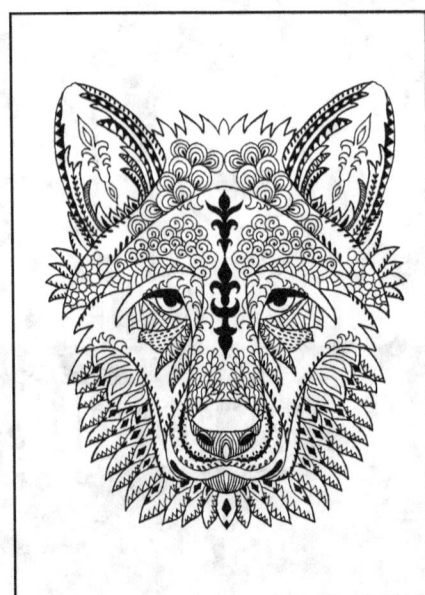
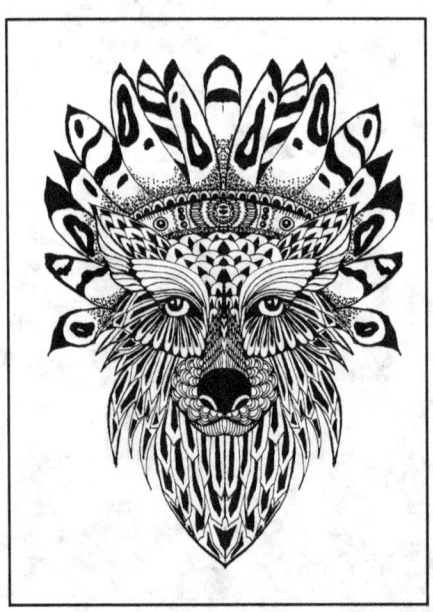

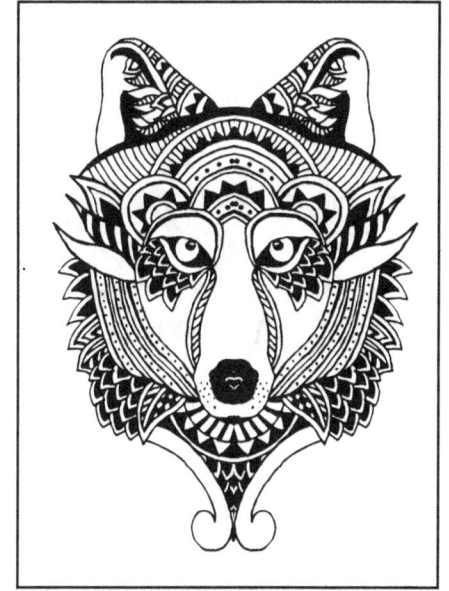
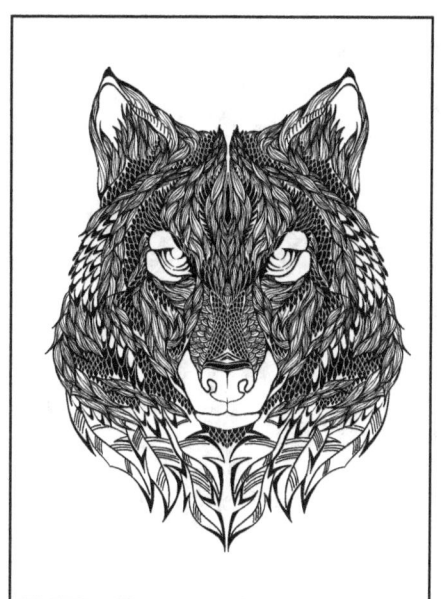
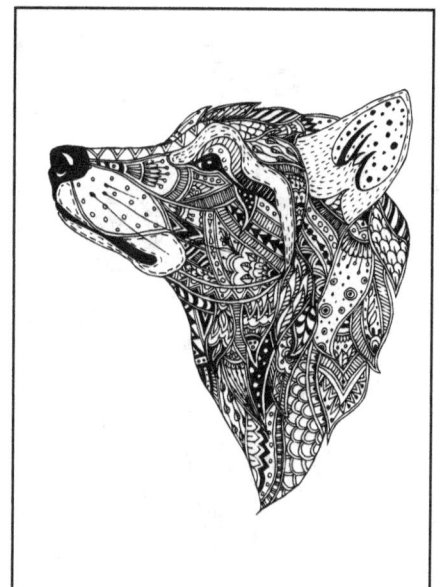
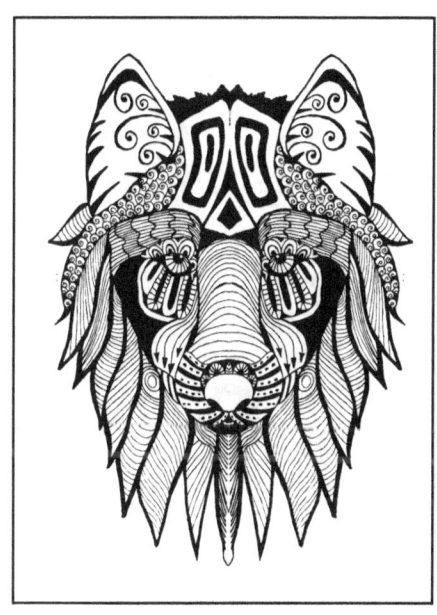
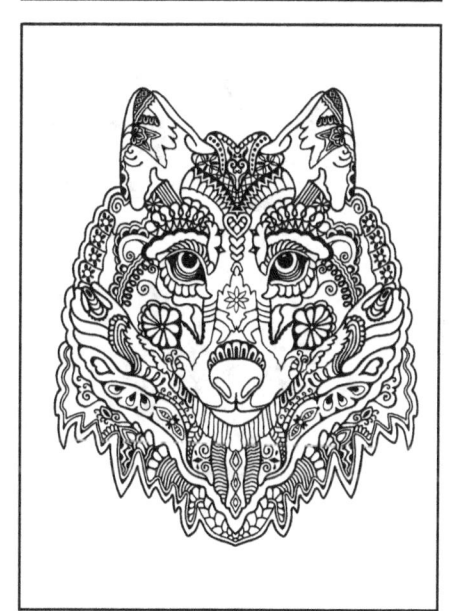
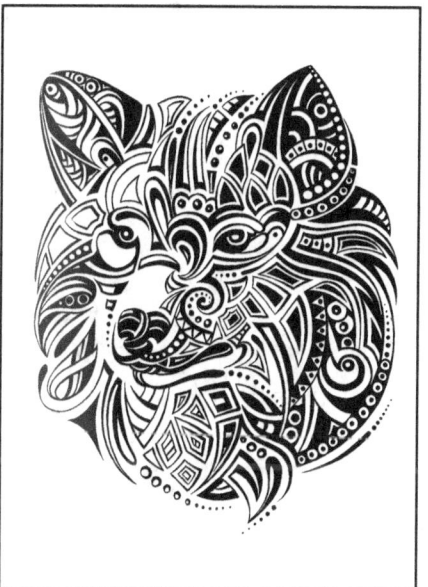
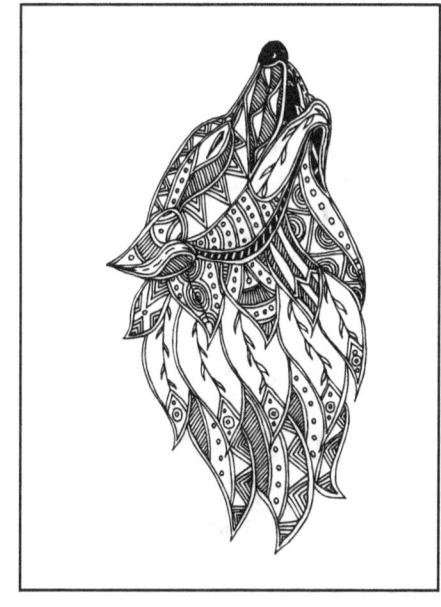
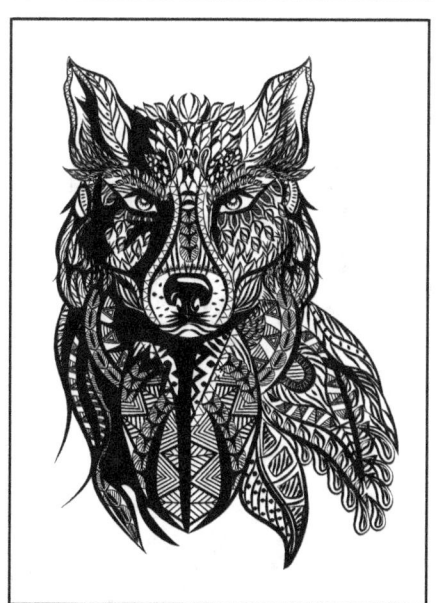
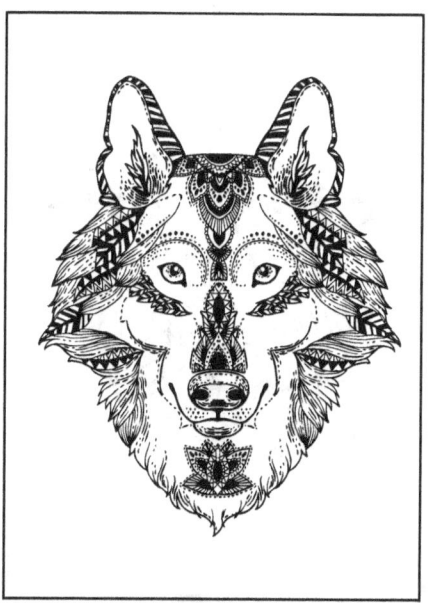

Preview of Coloring Pages

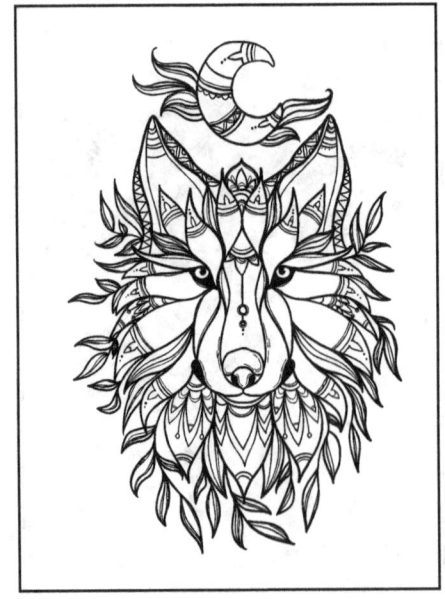
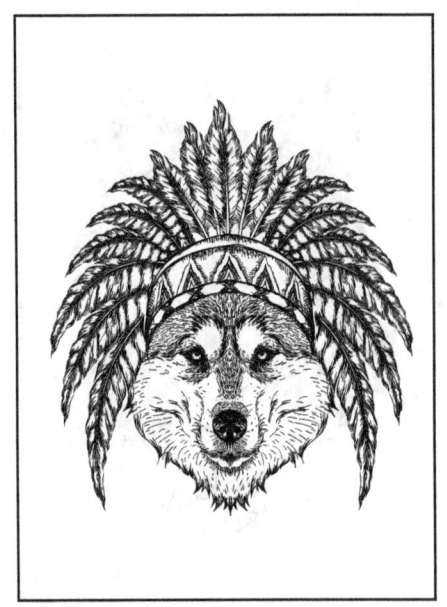
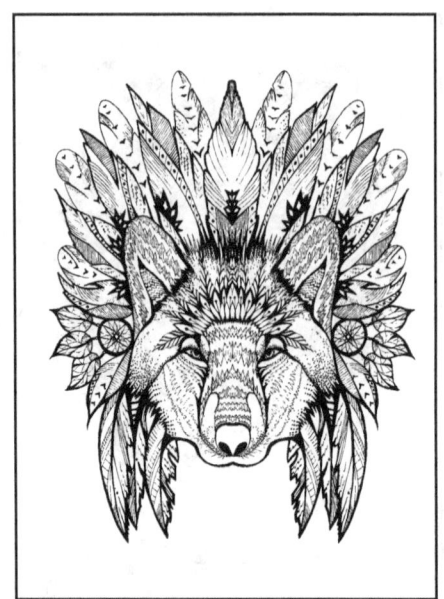
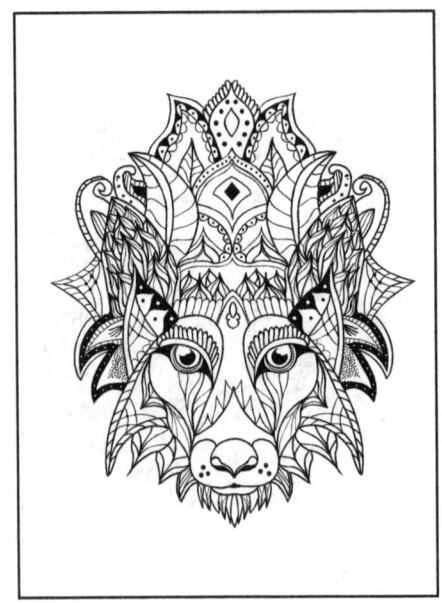
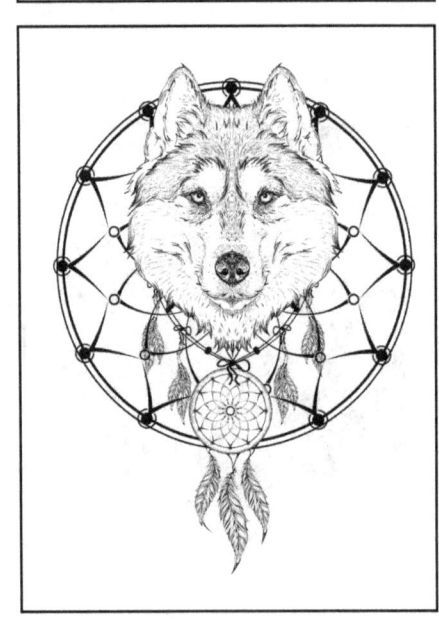
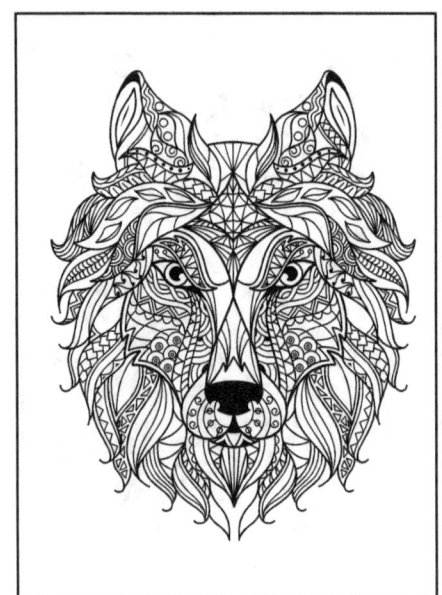
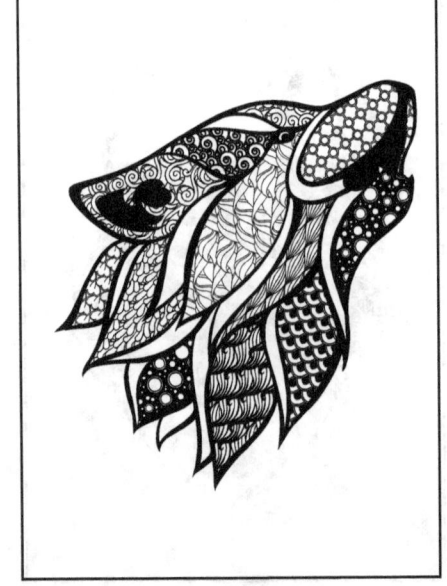
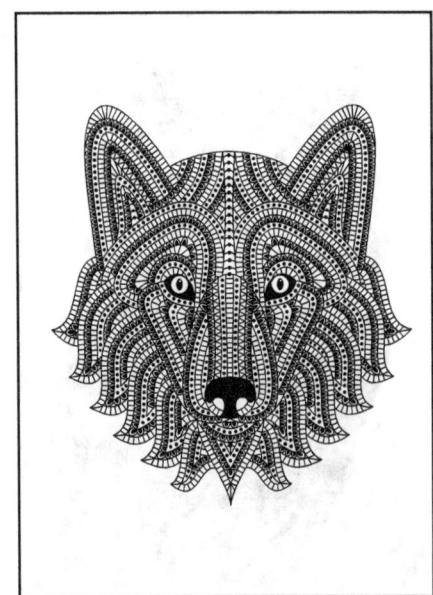
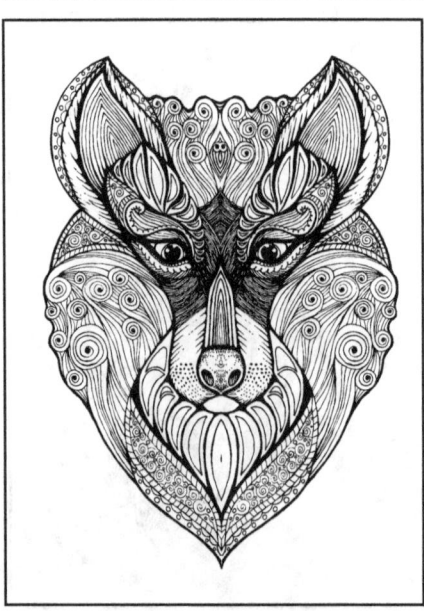

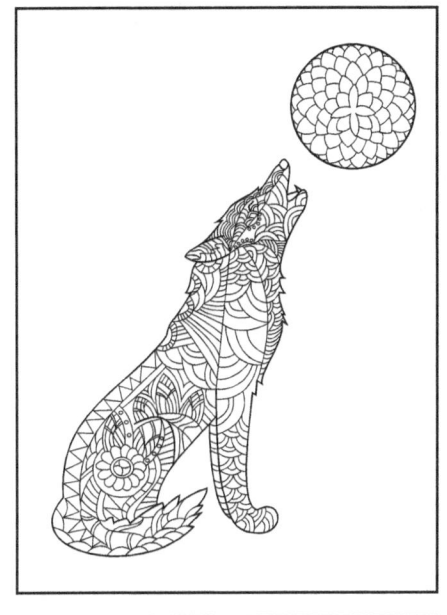
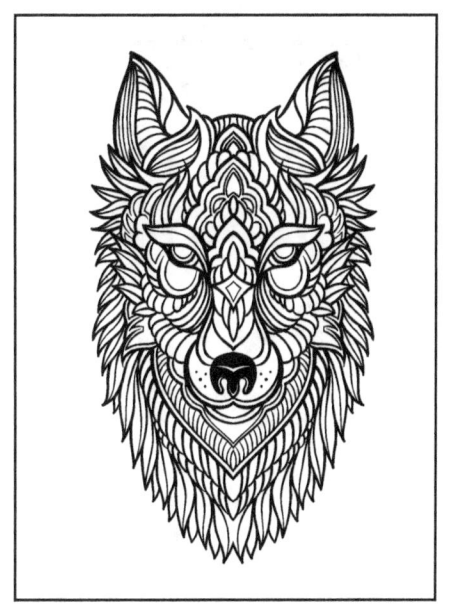
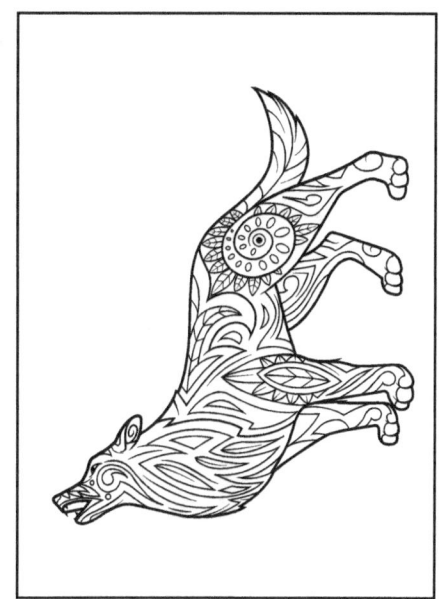
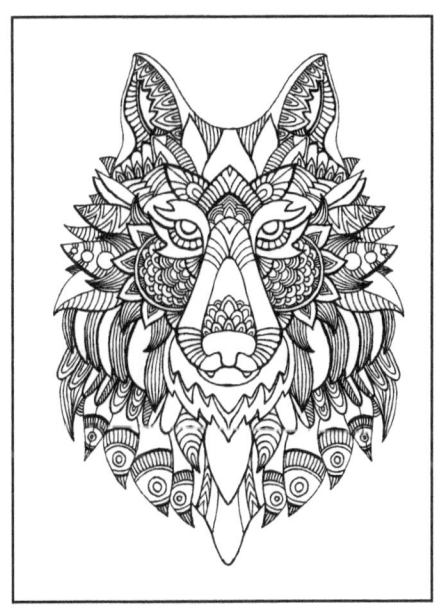
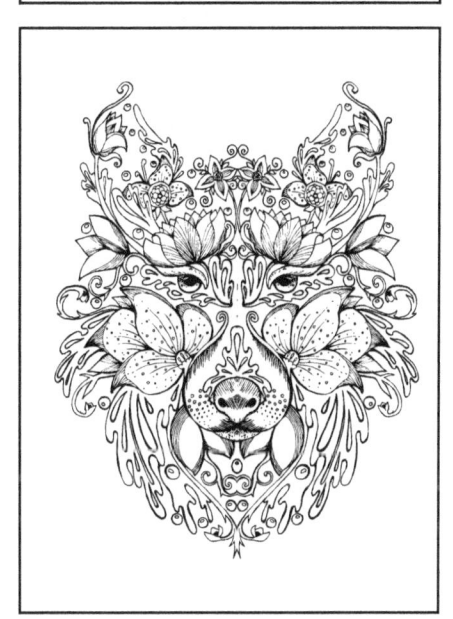
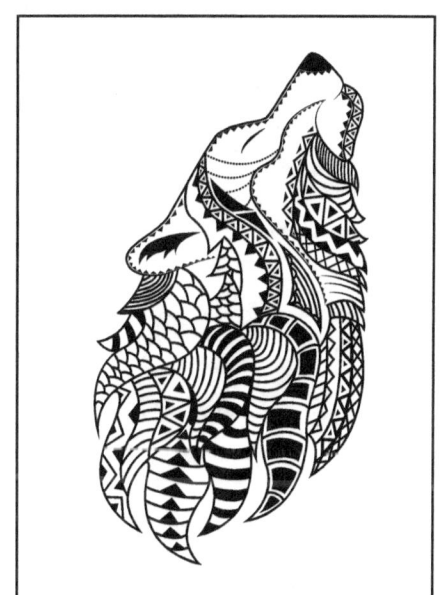
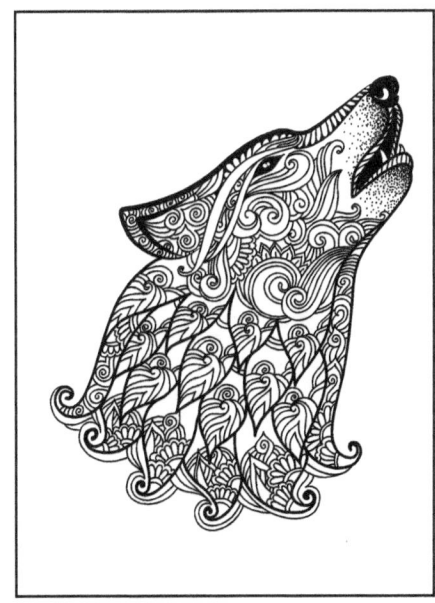
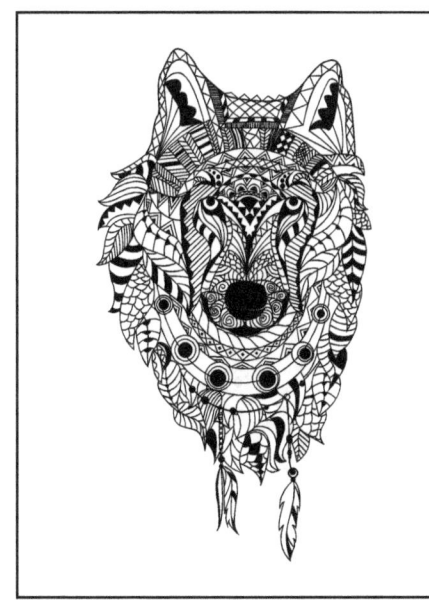
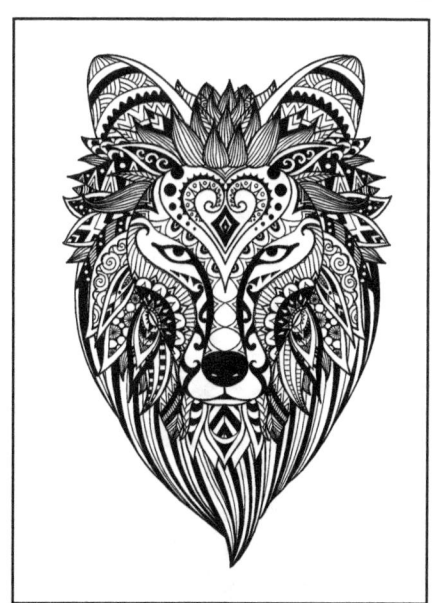

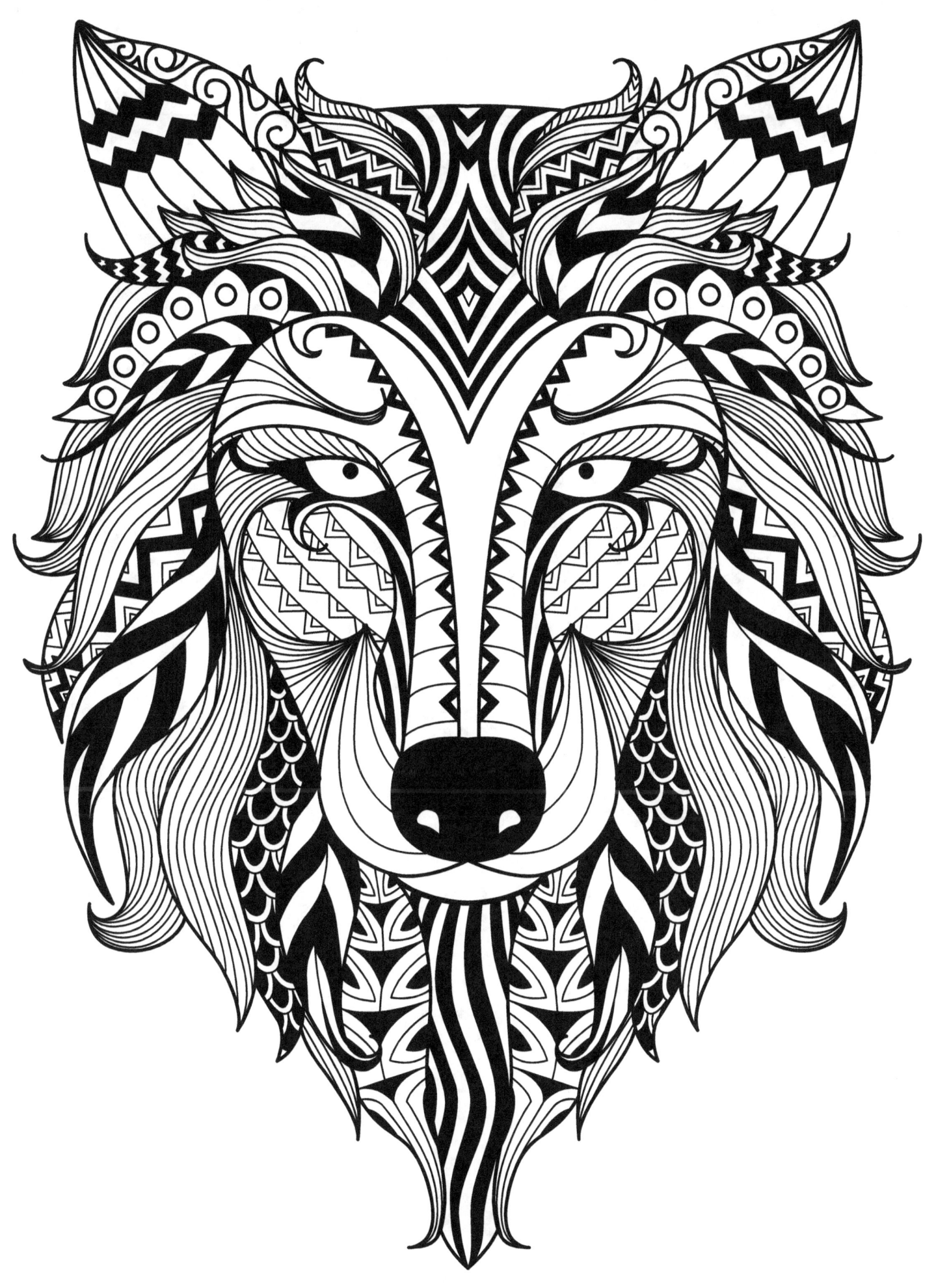

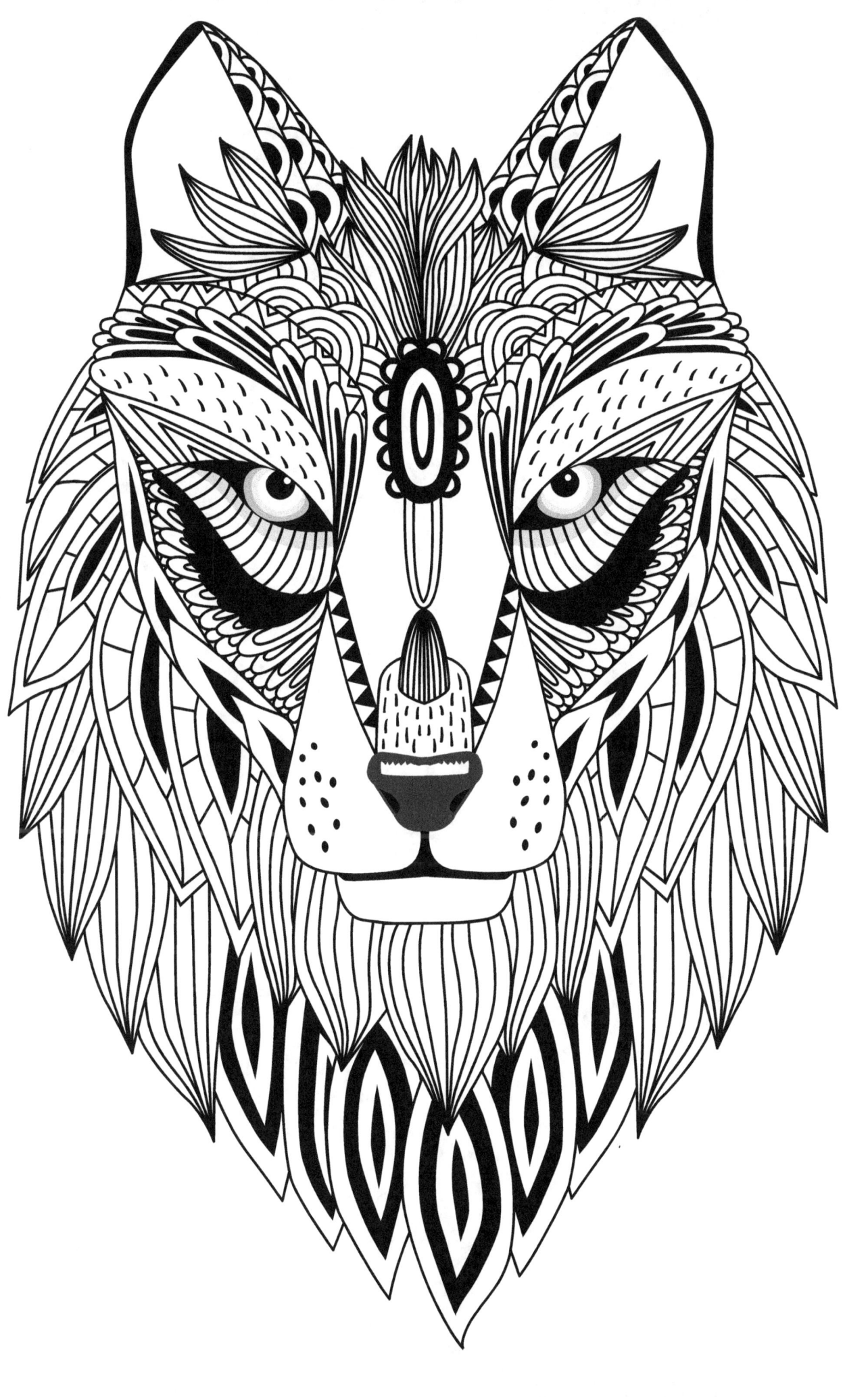

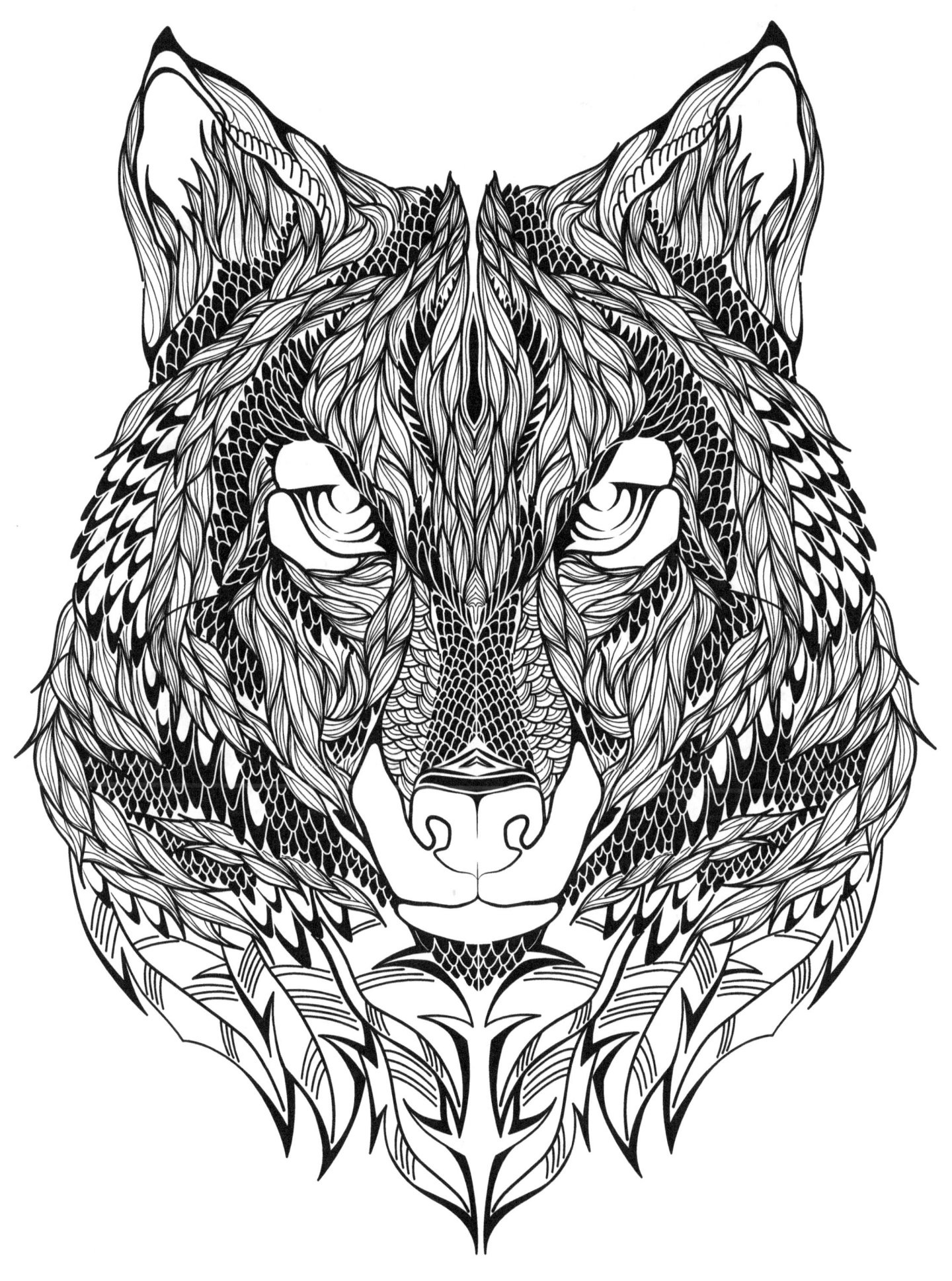

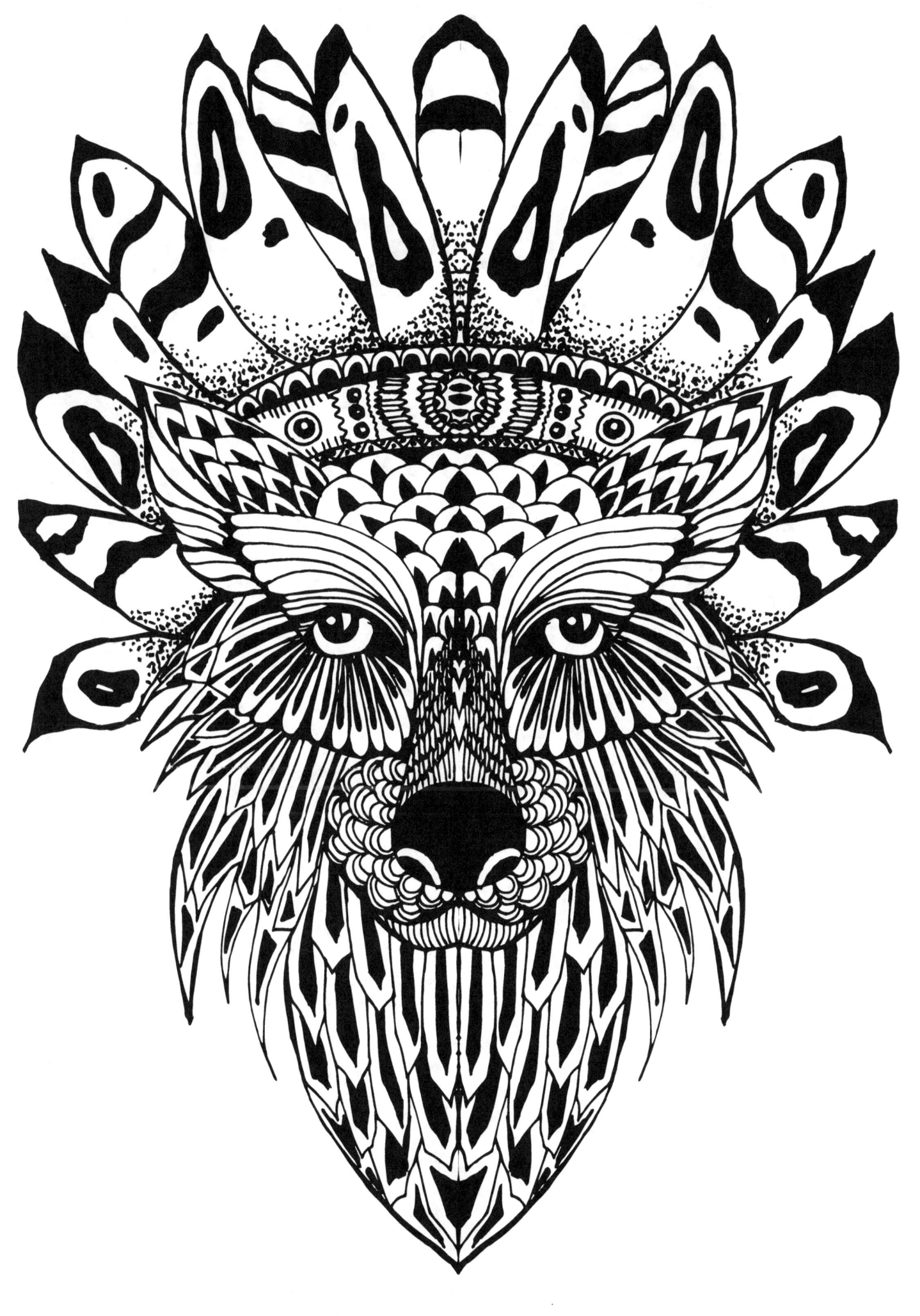

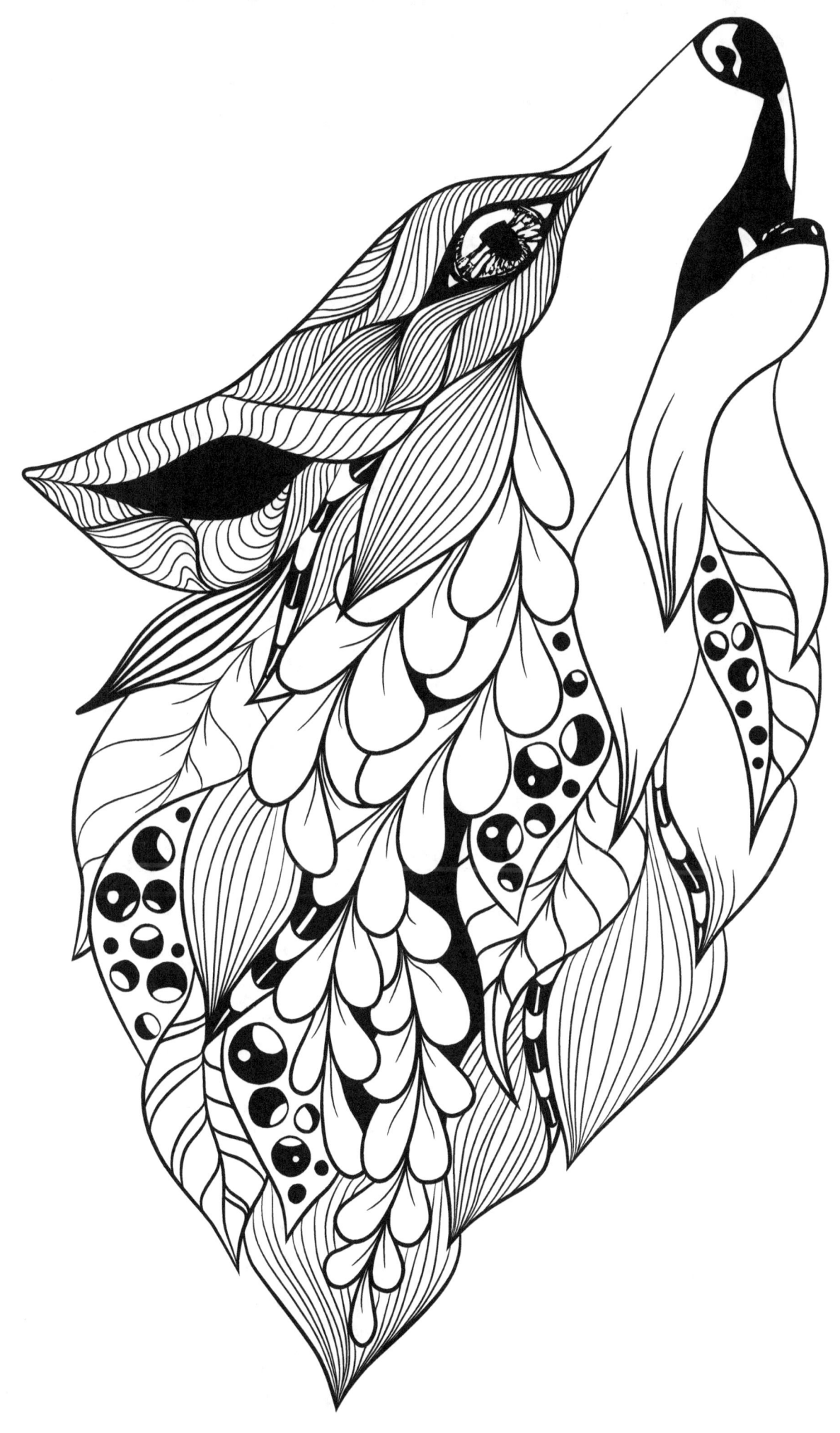

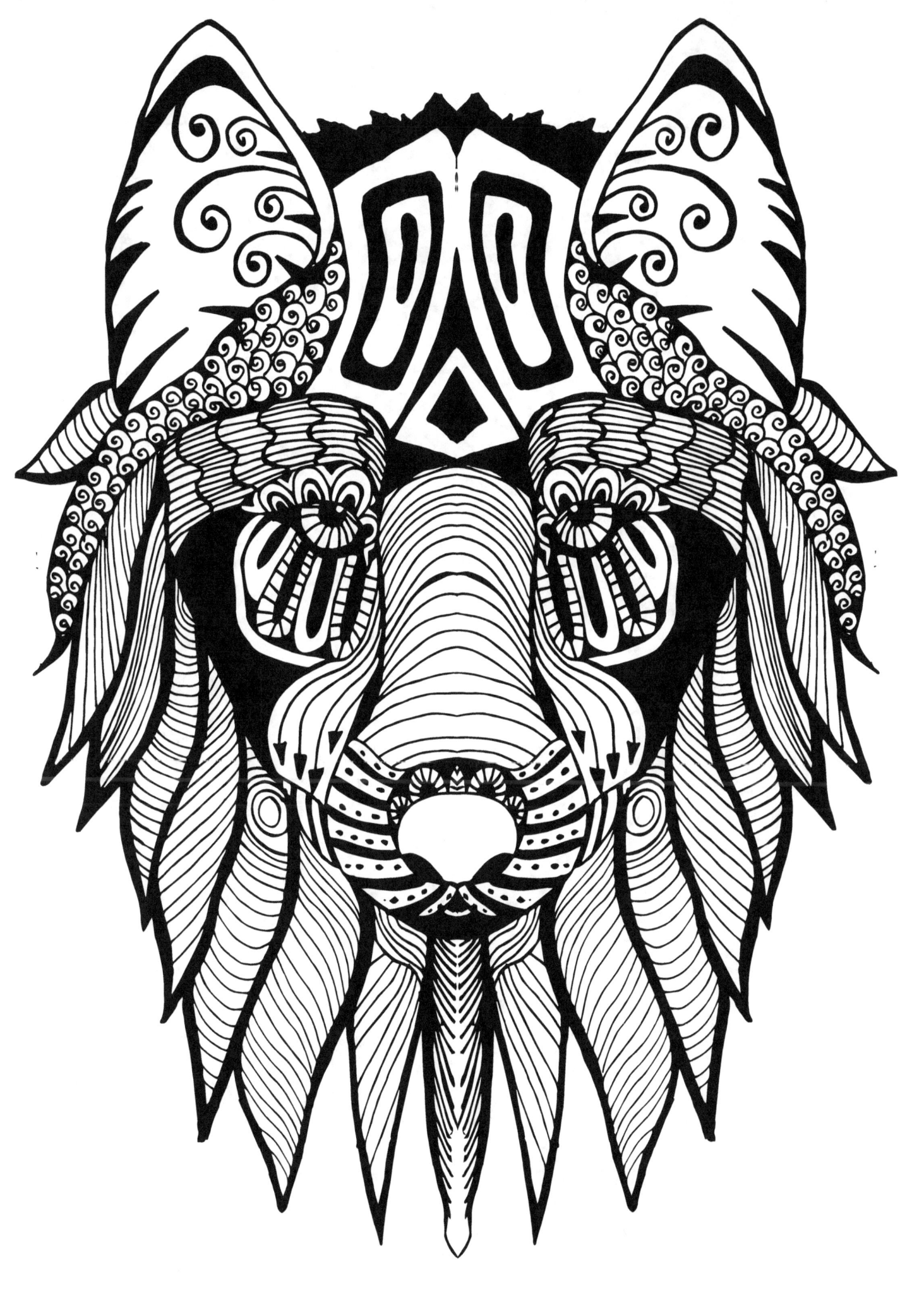

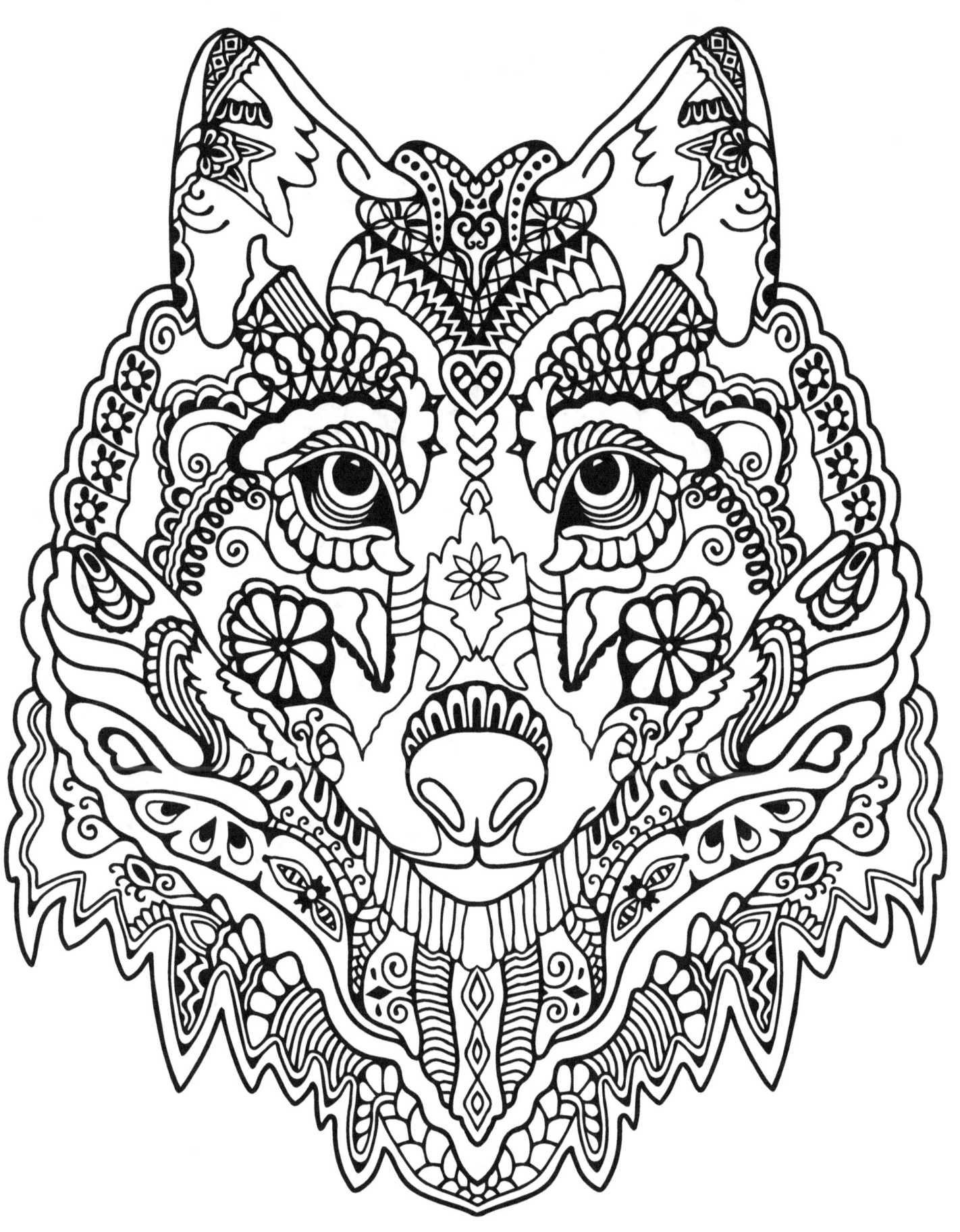

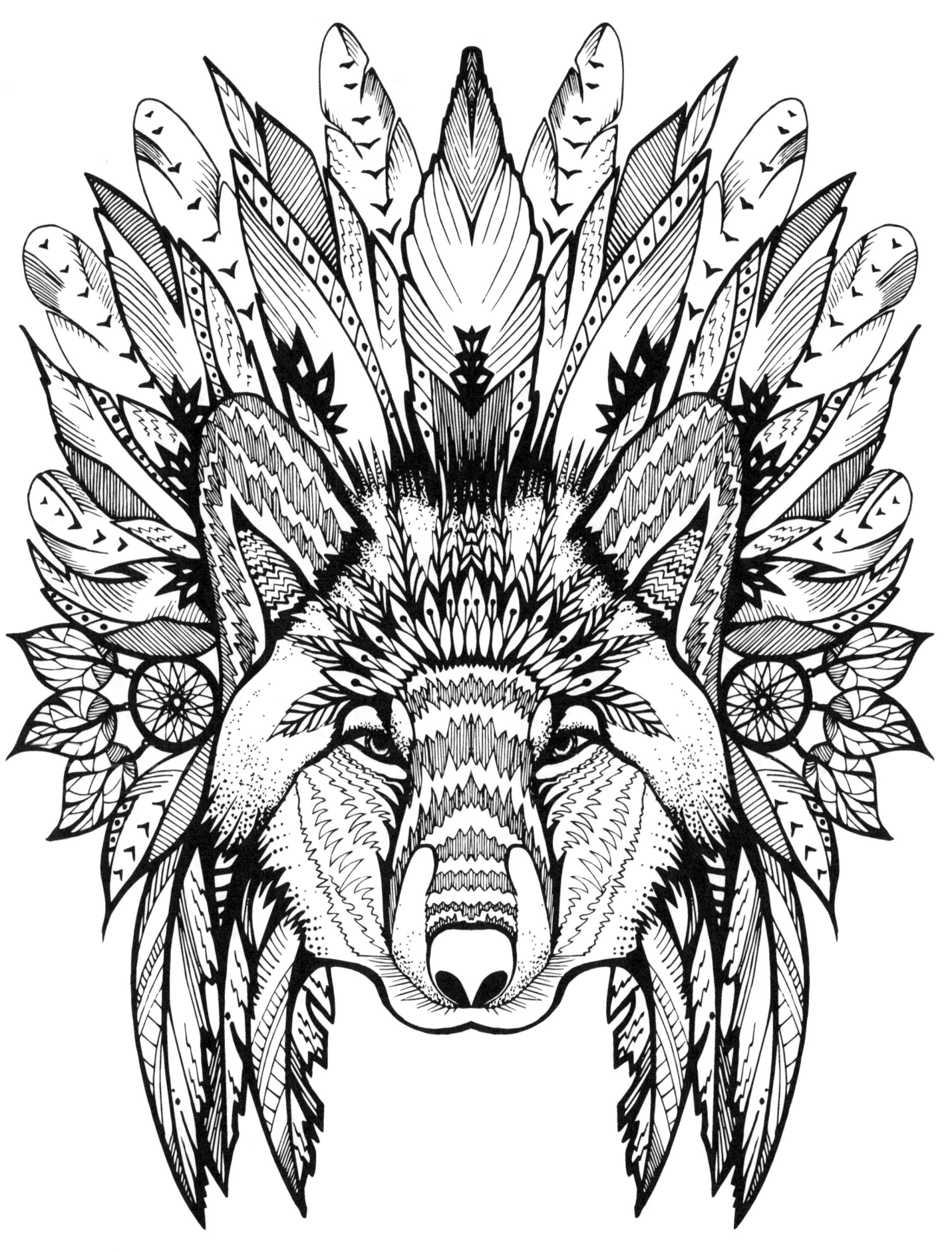

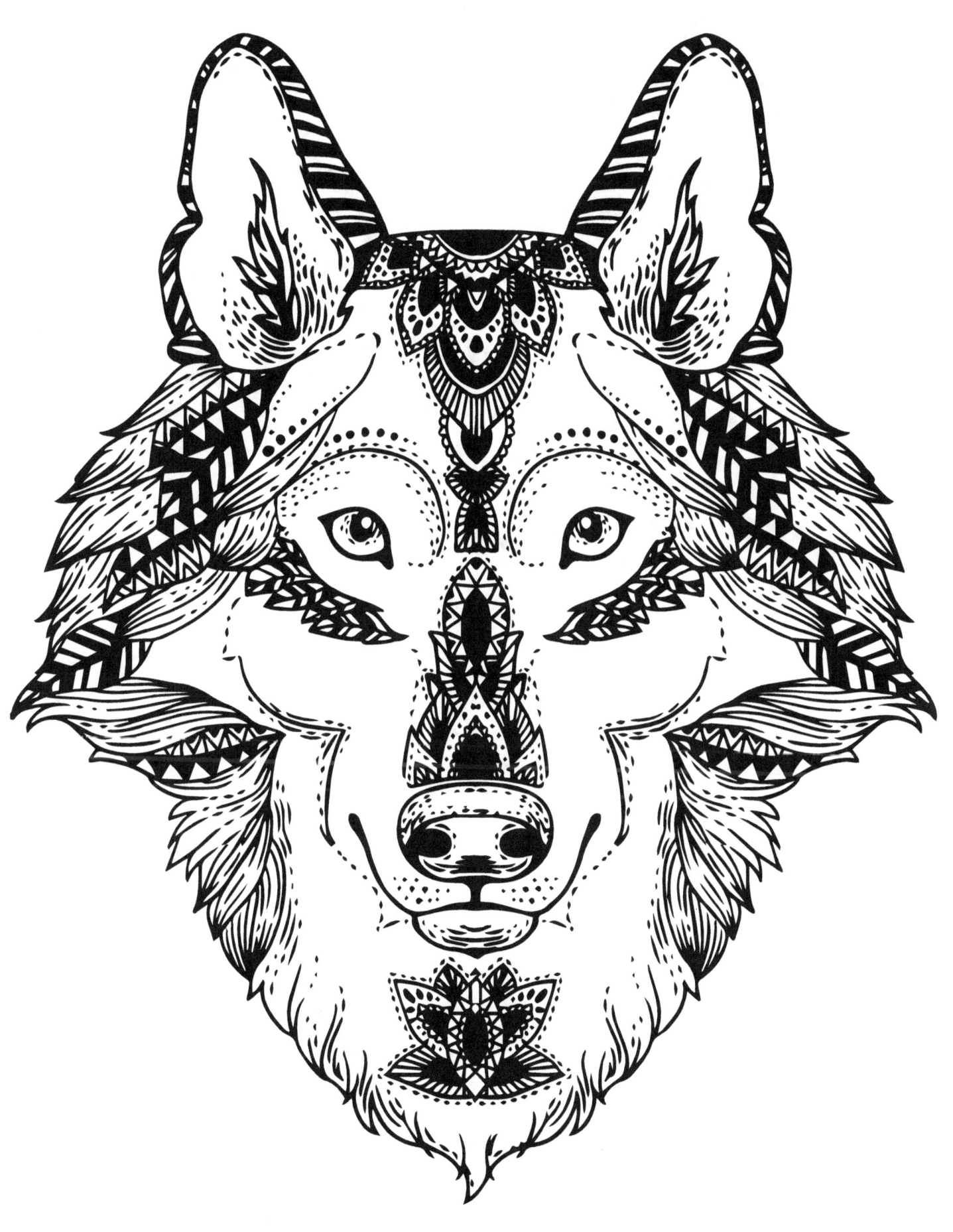

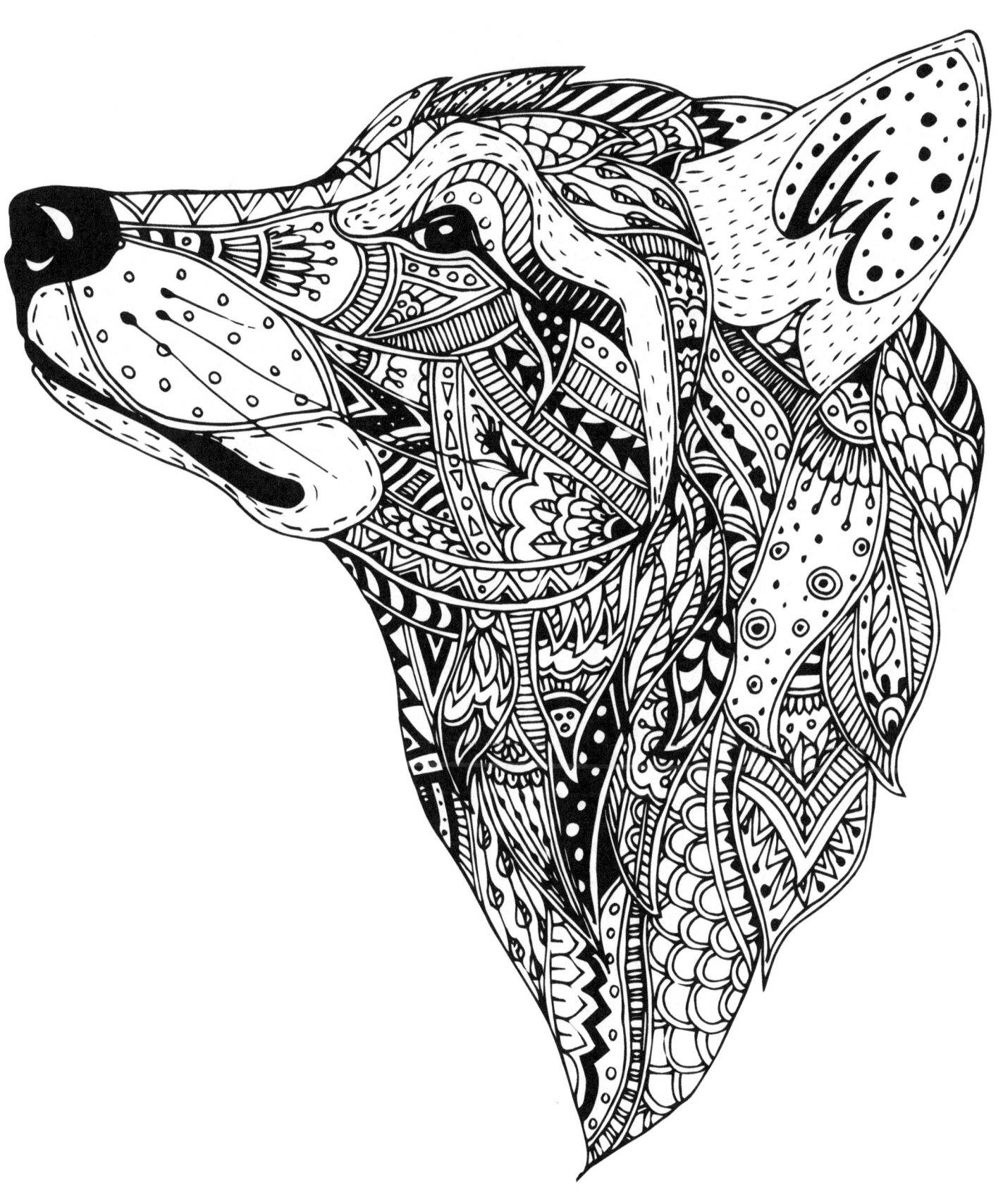

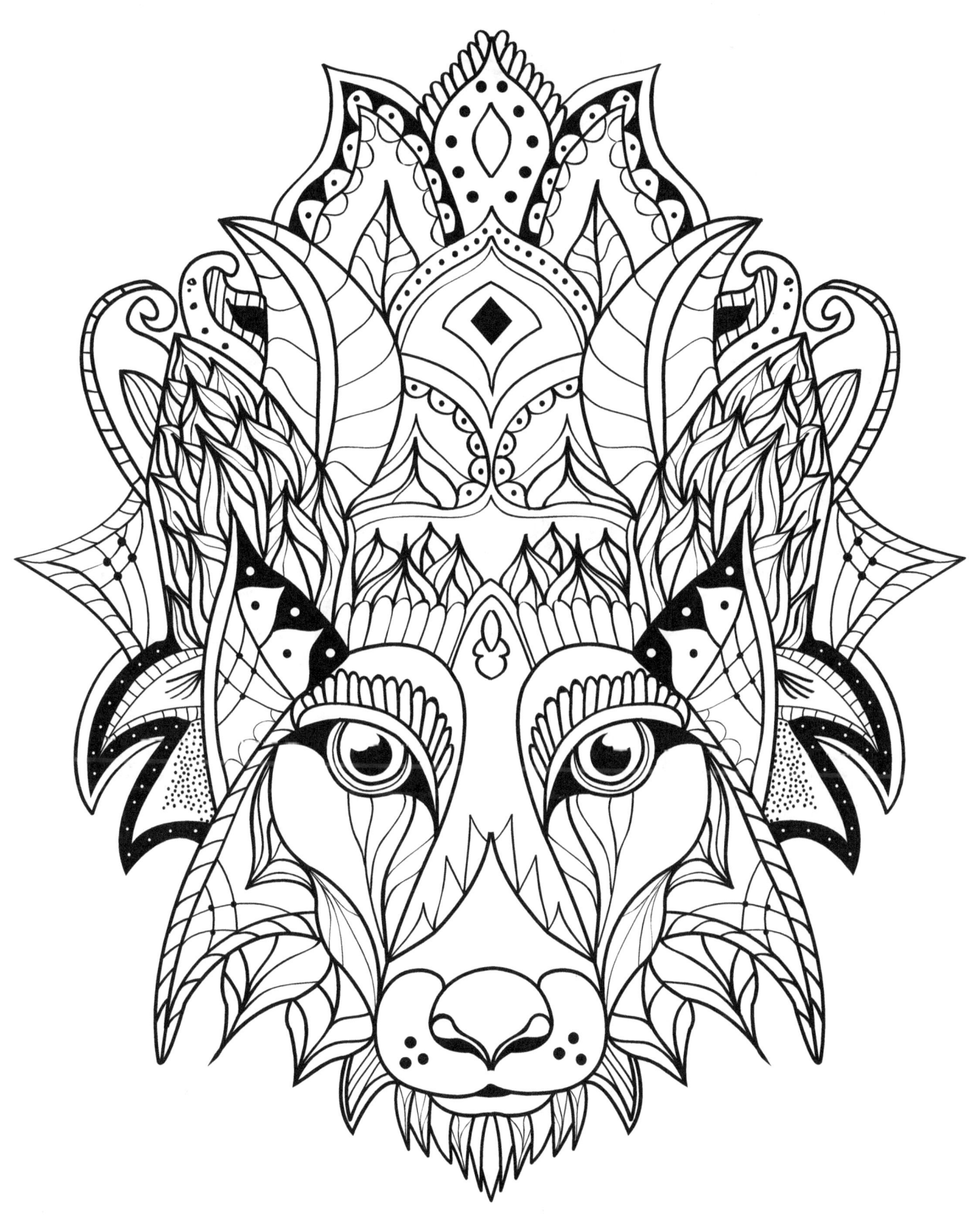

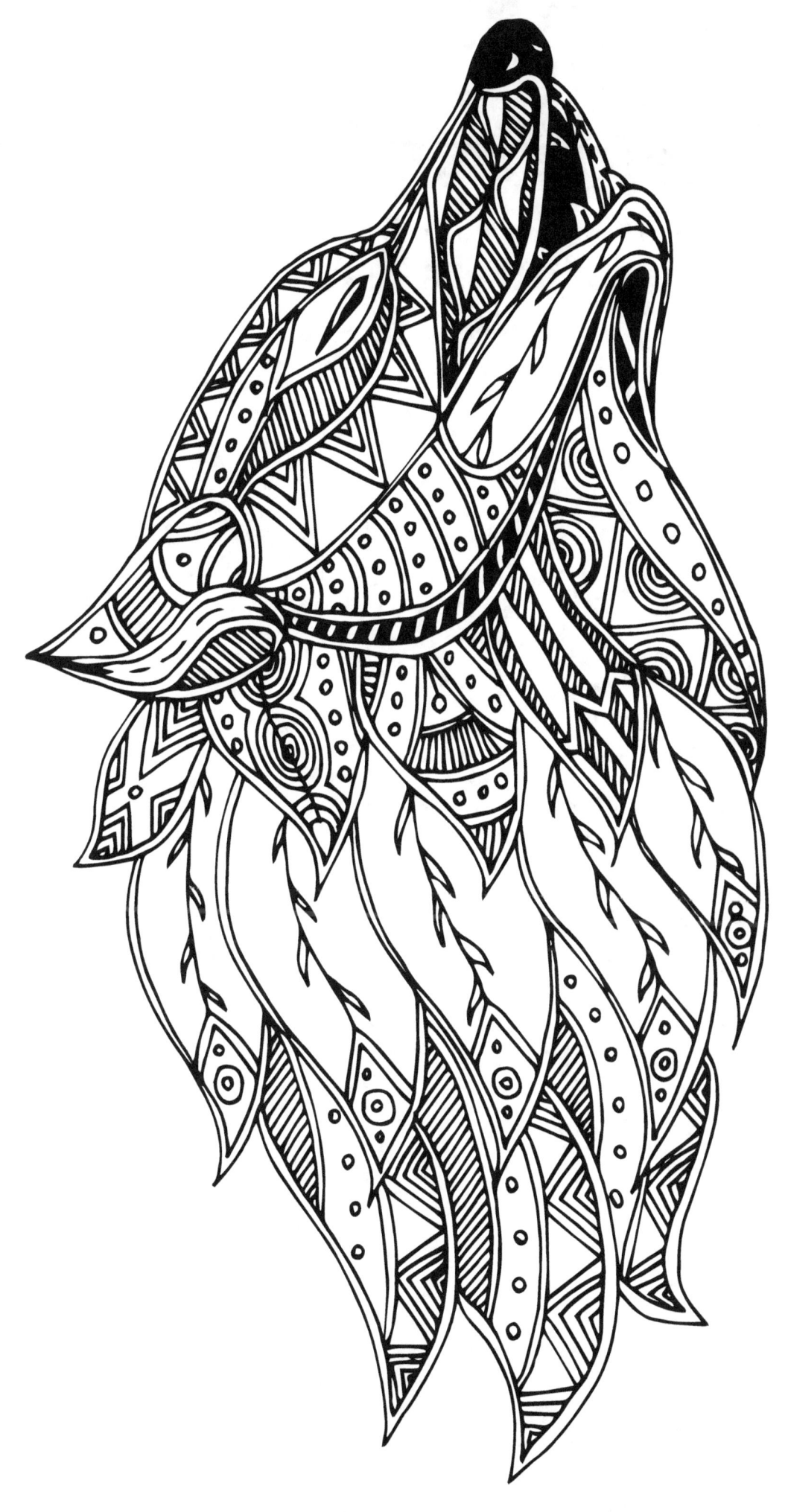

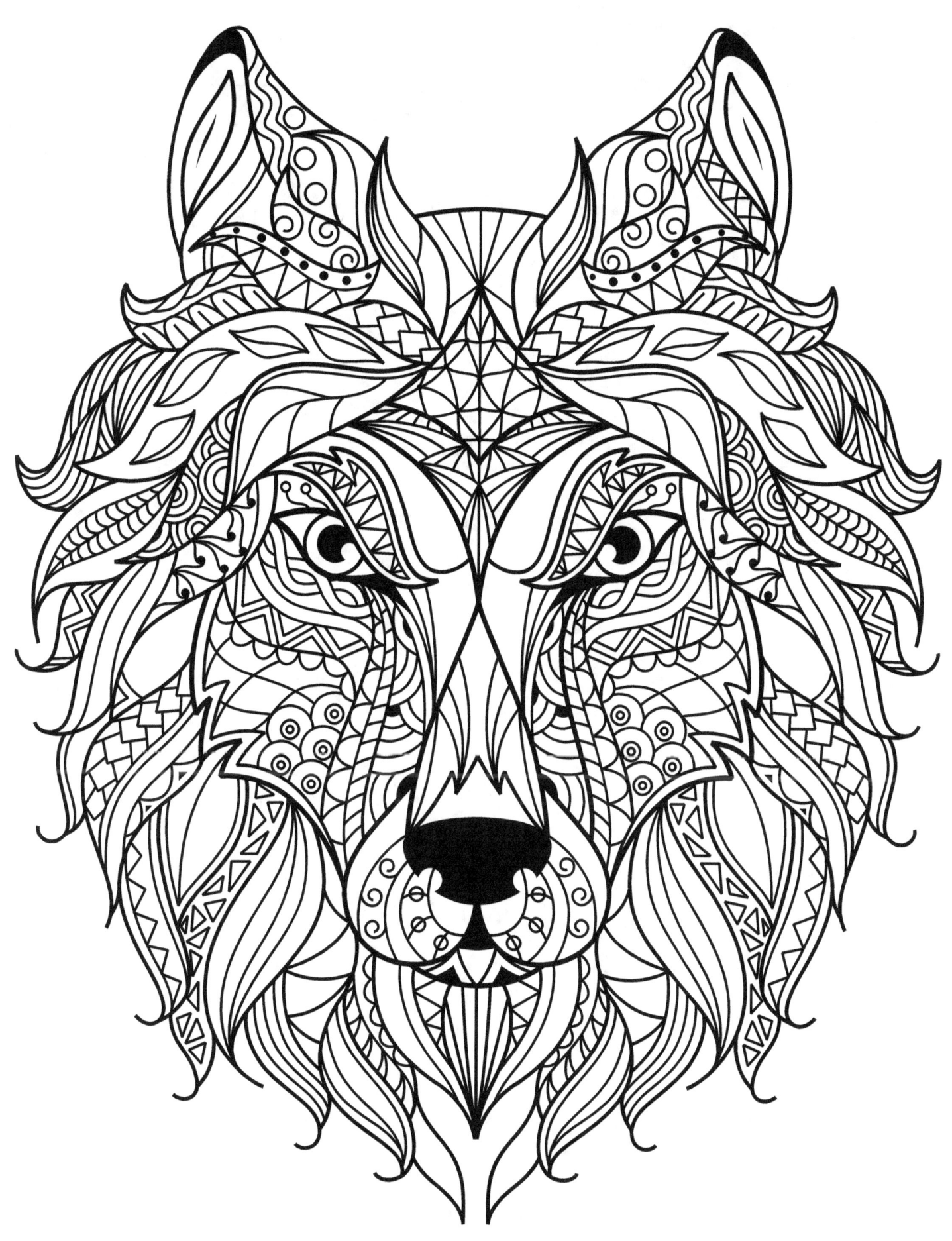

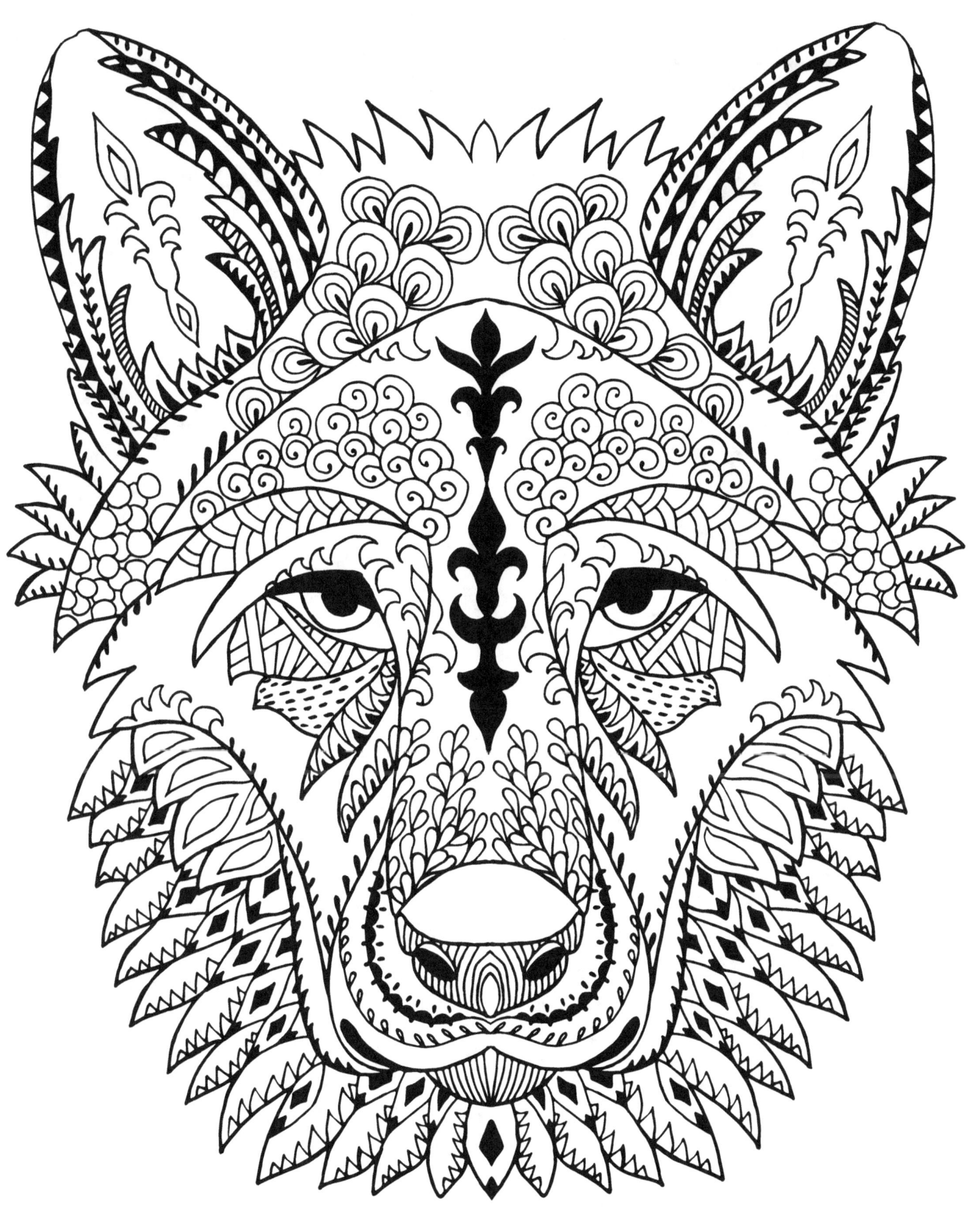

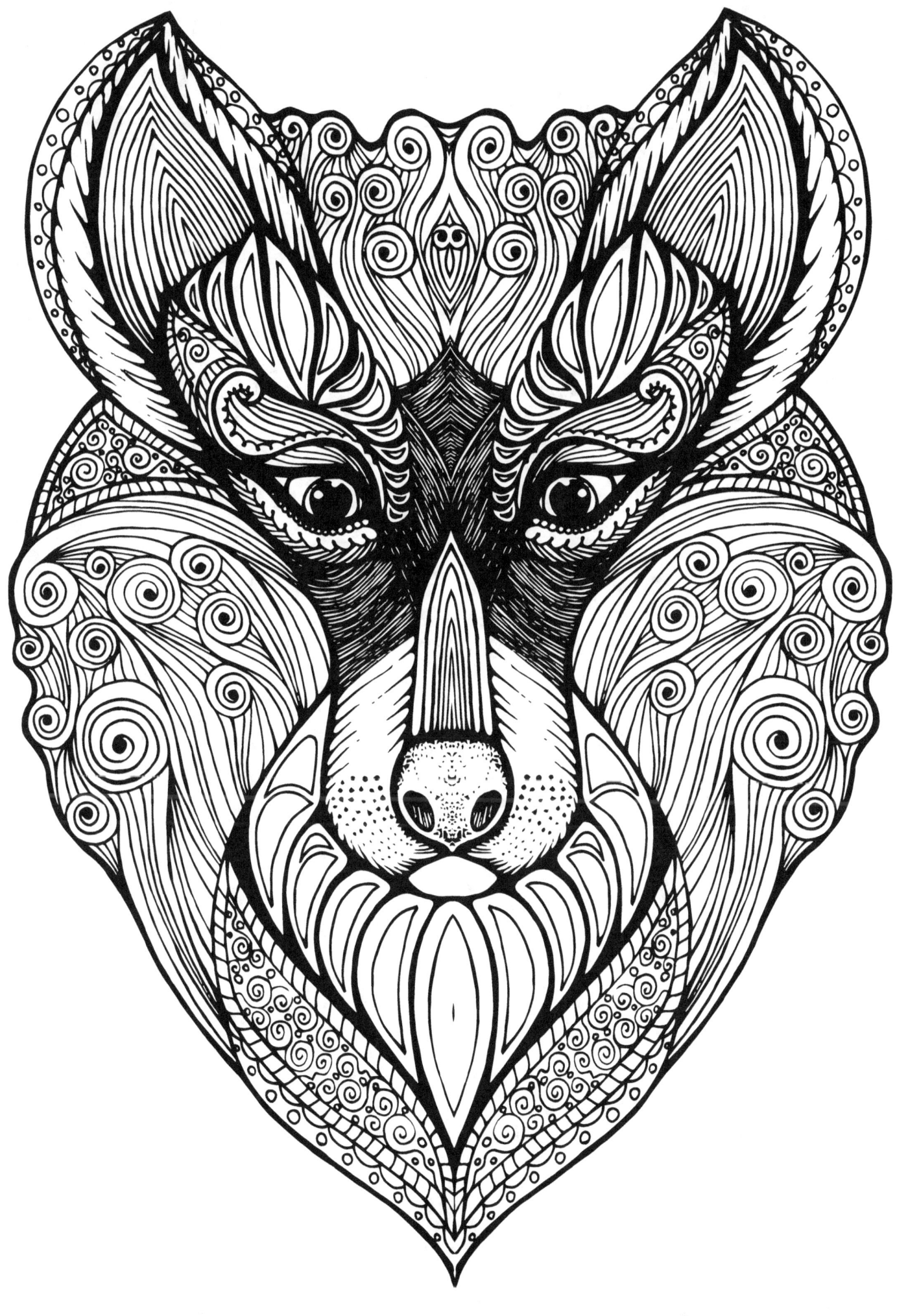

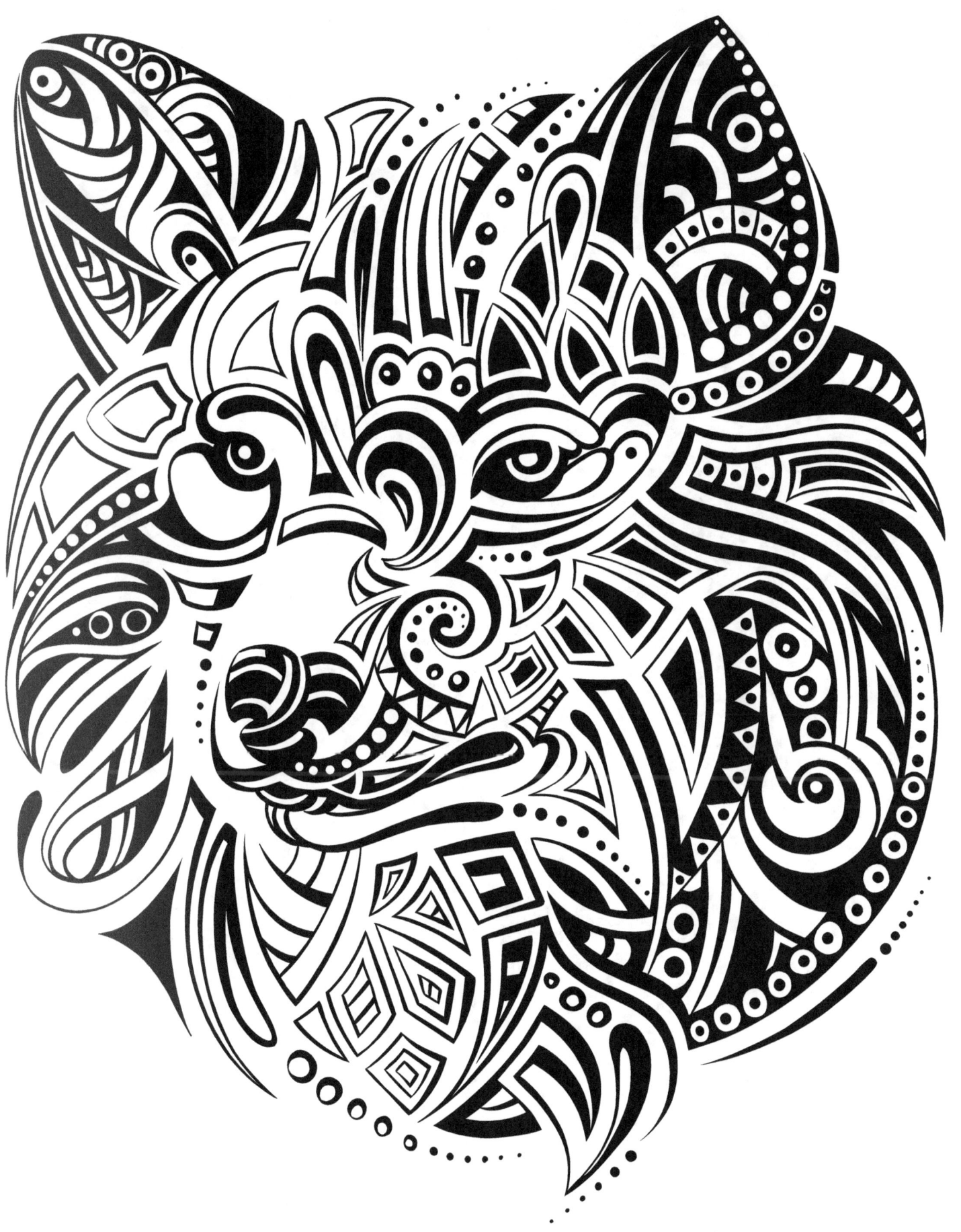

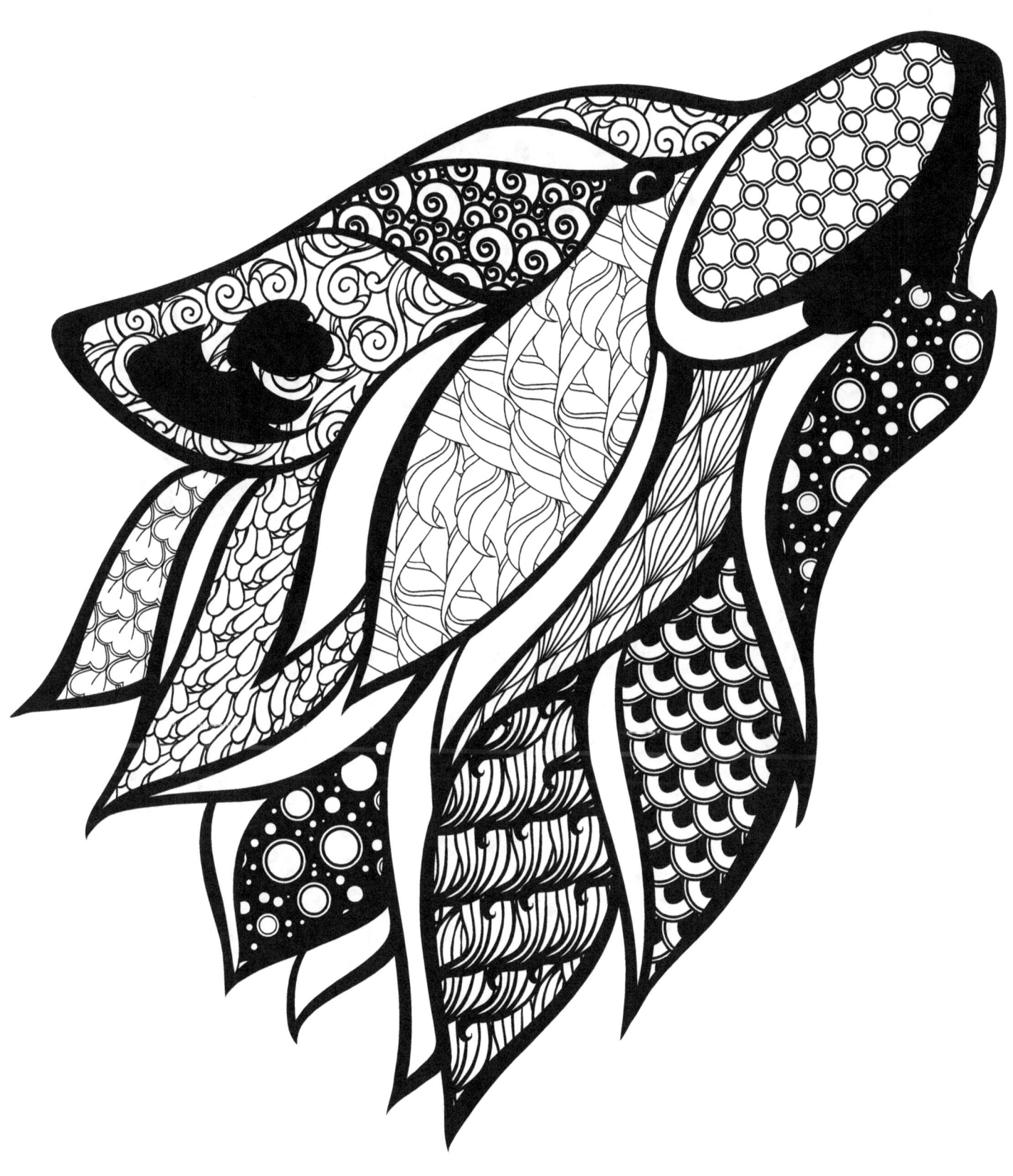

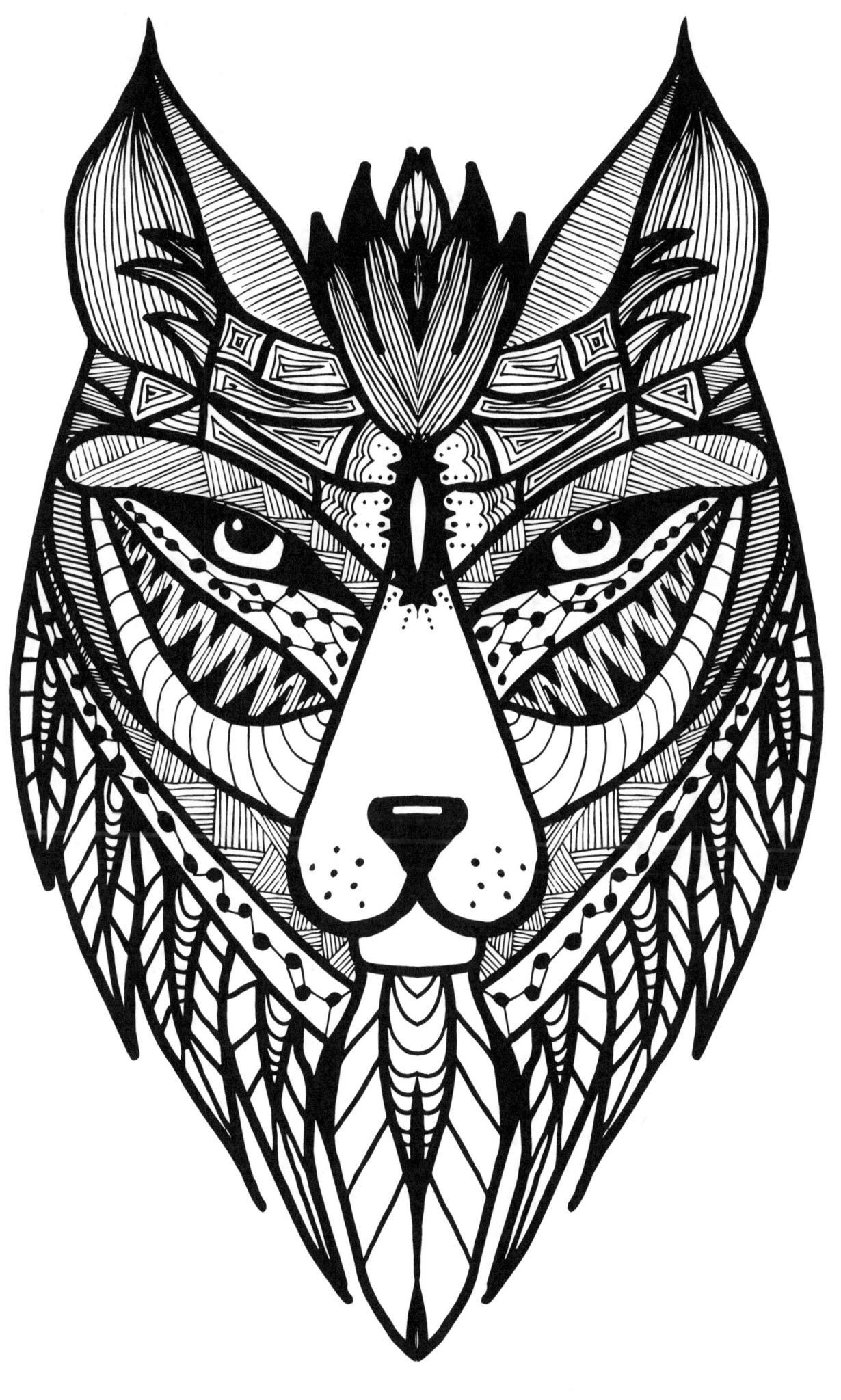

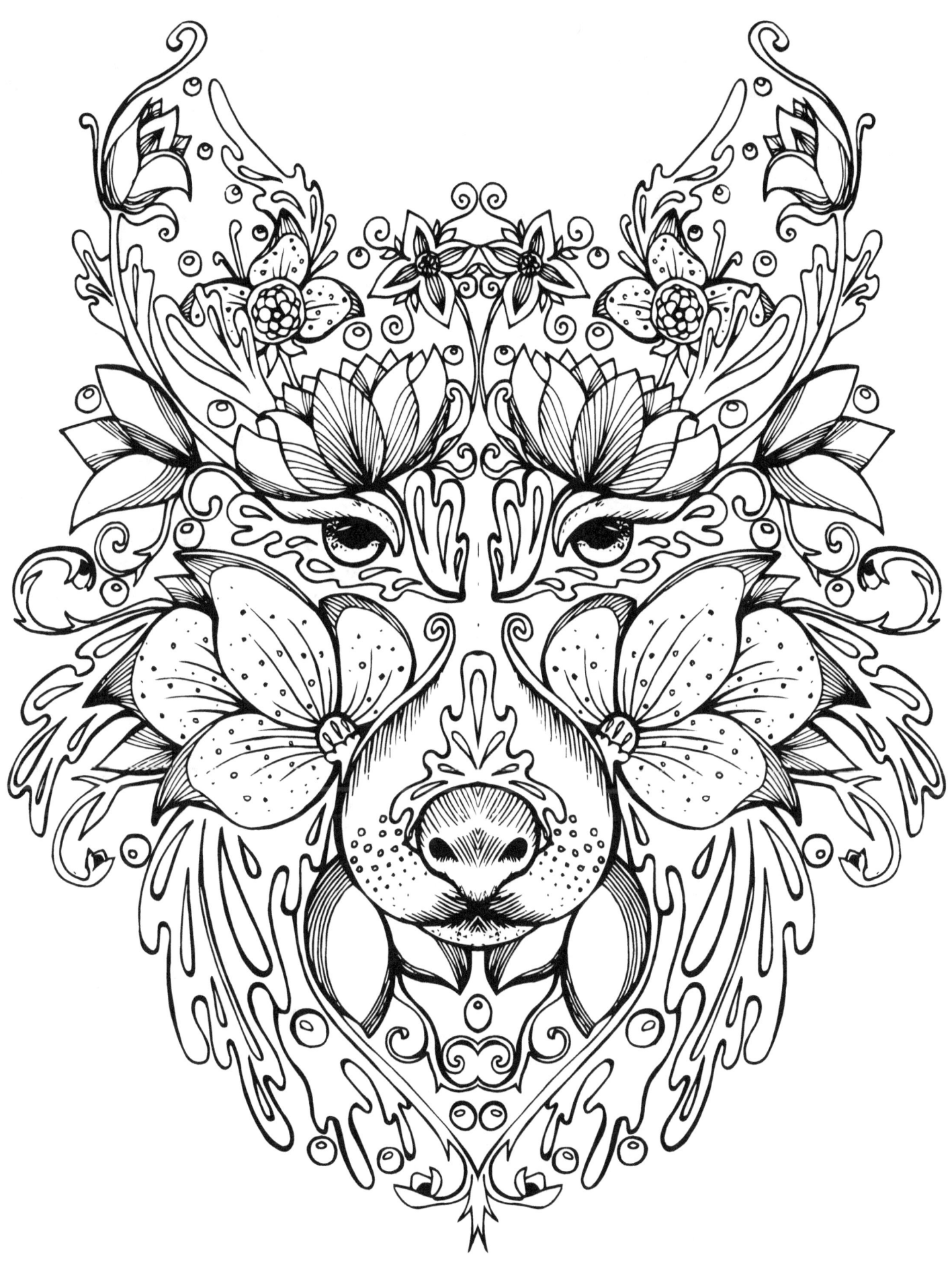

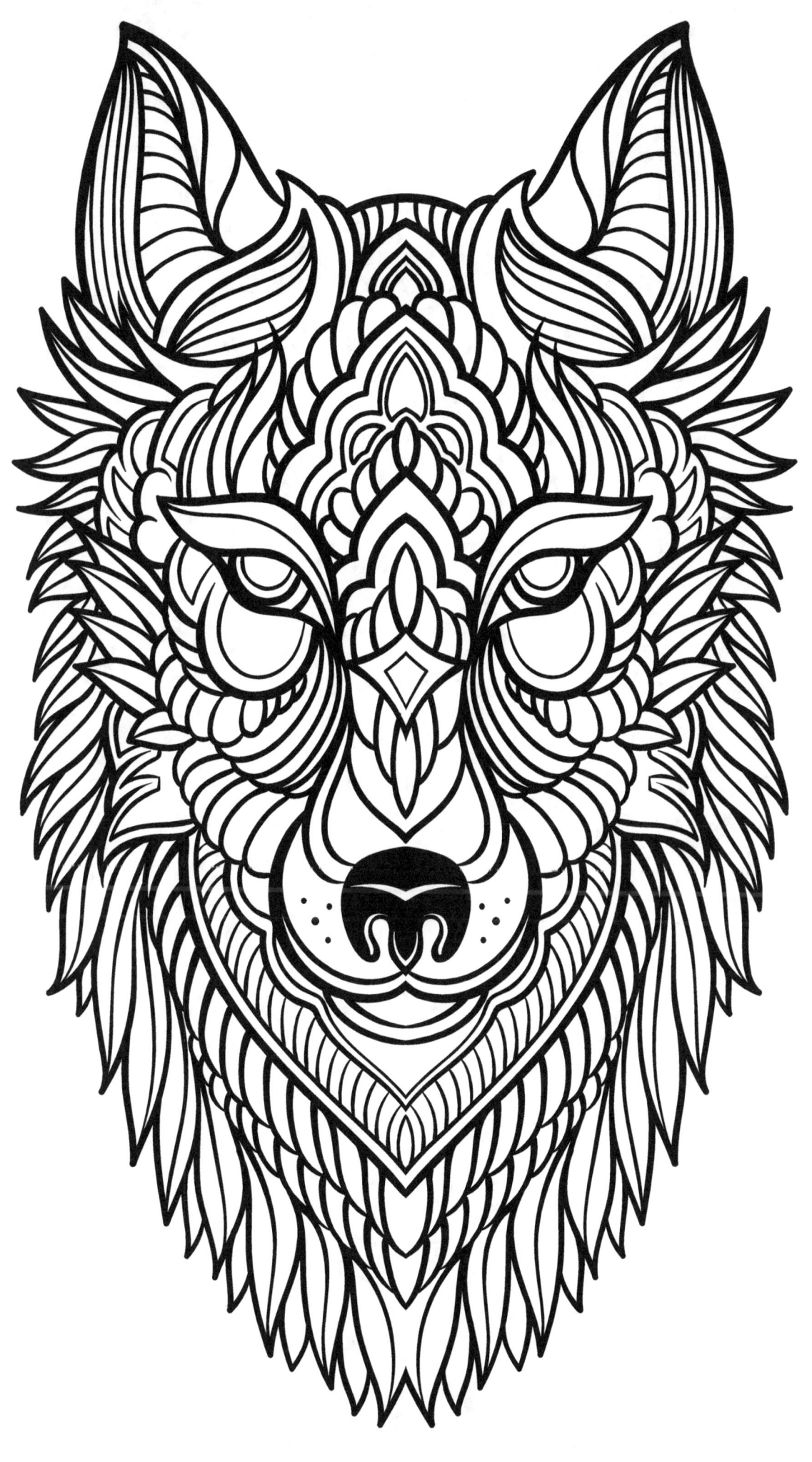

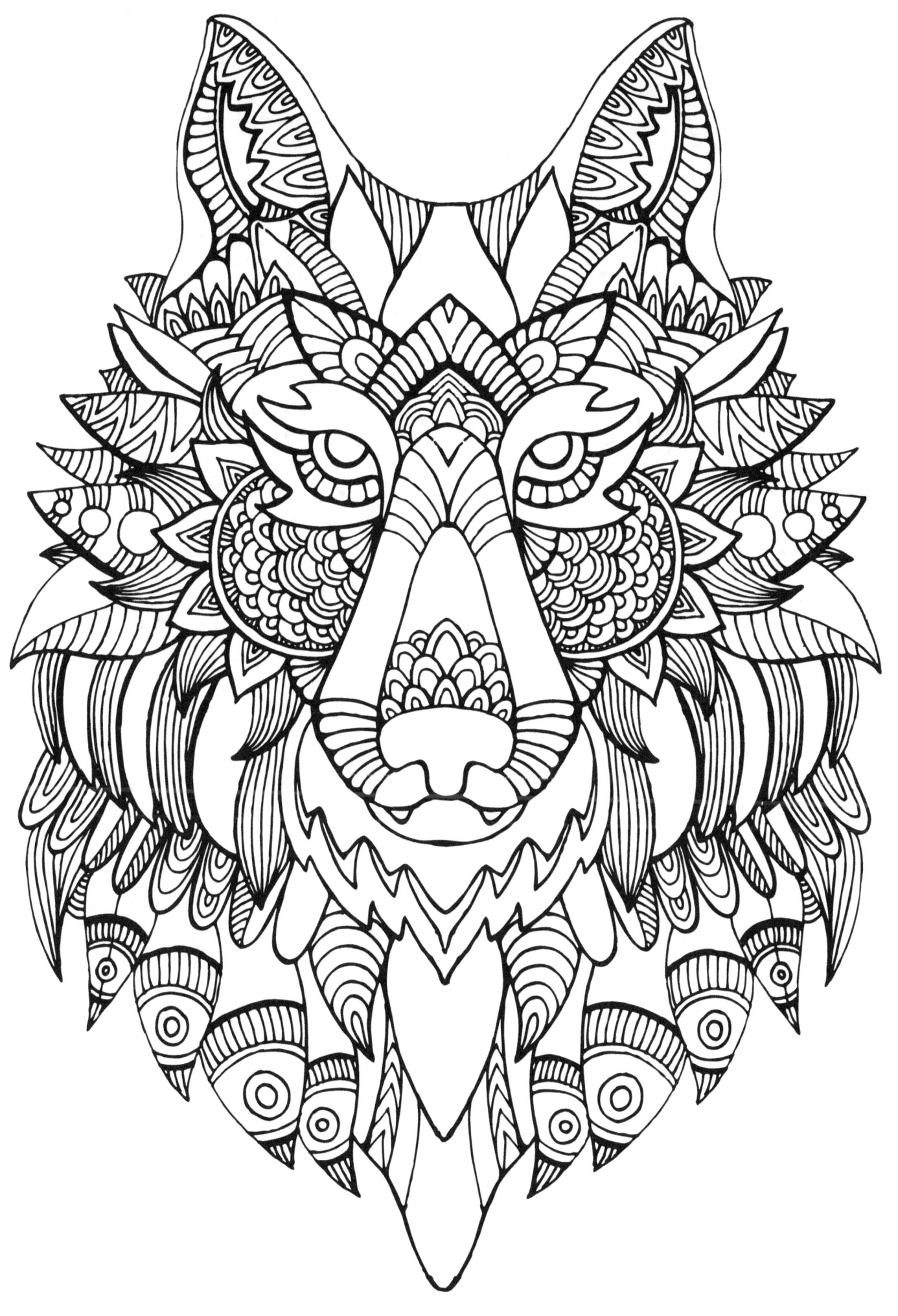

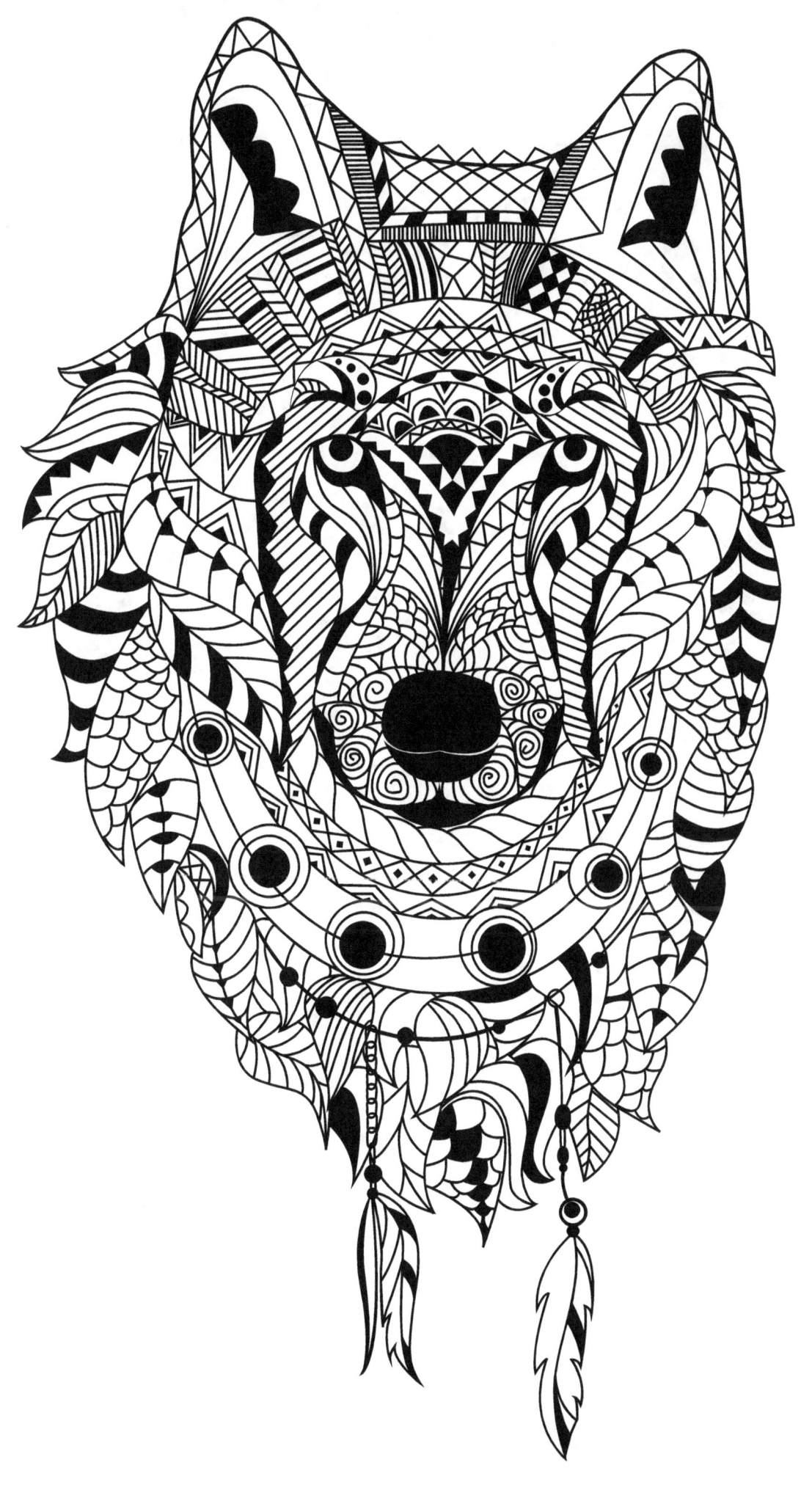

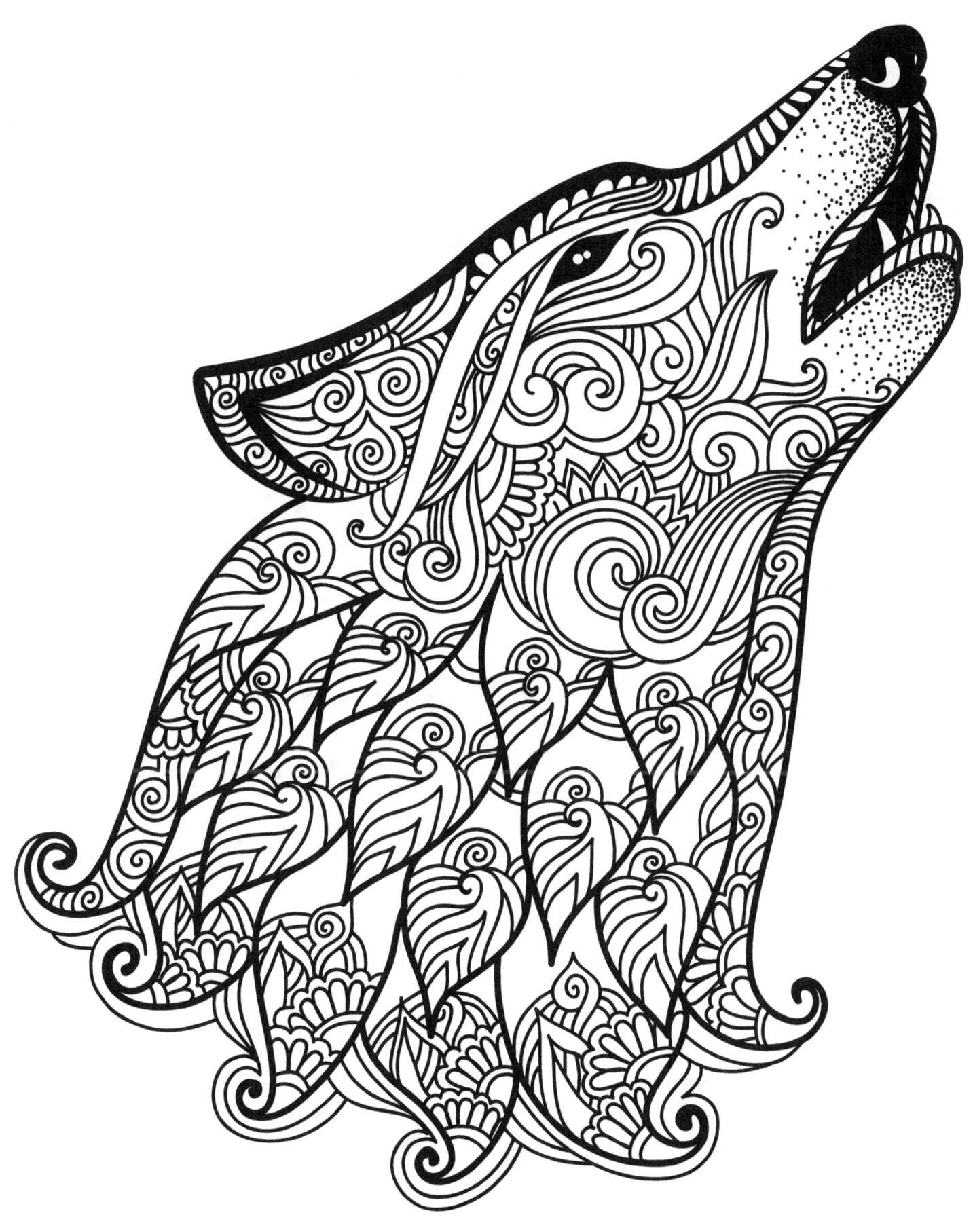

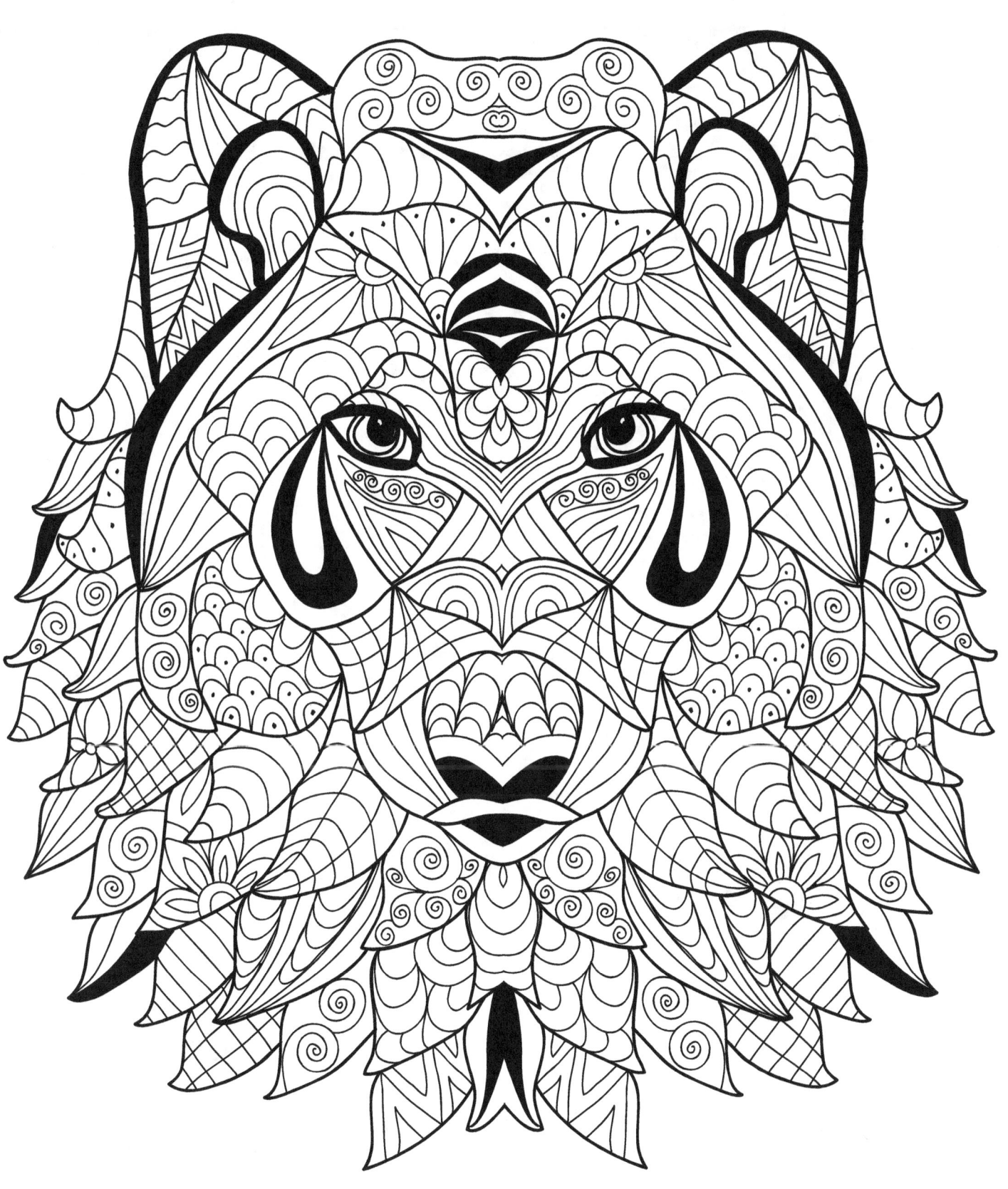

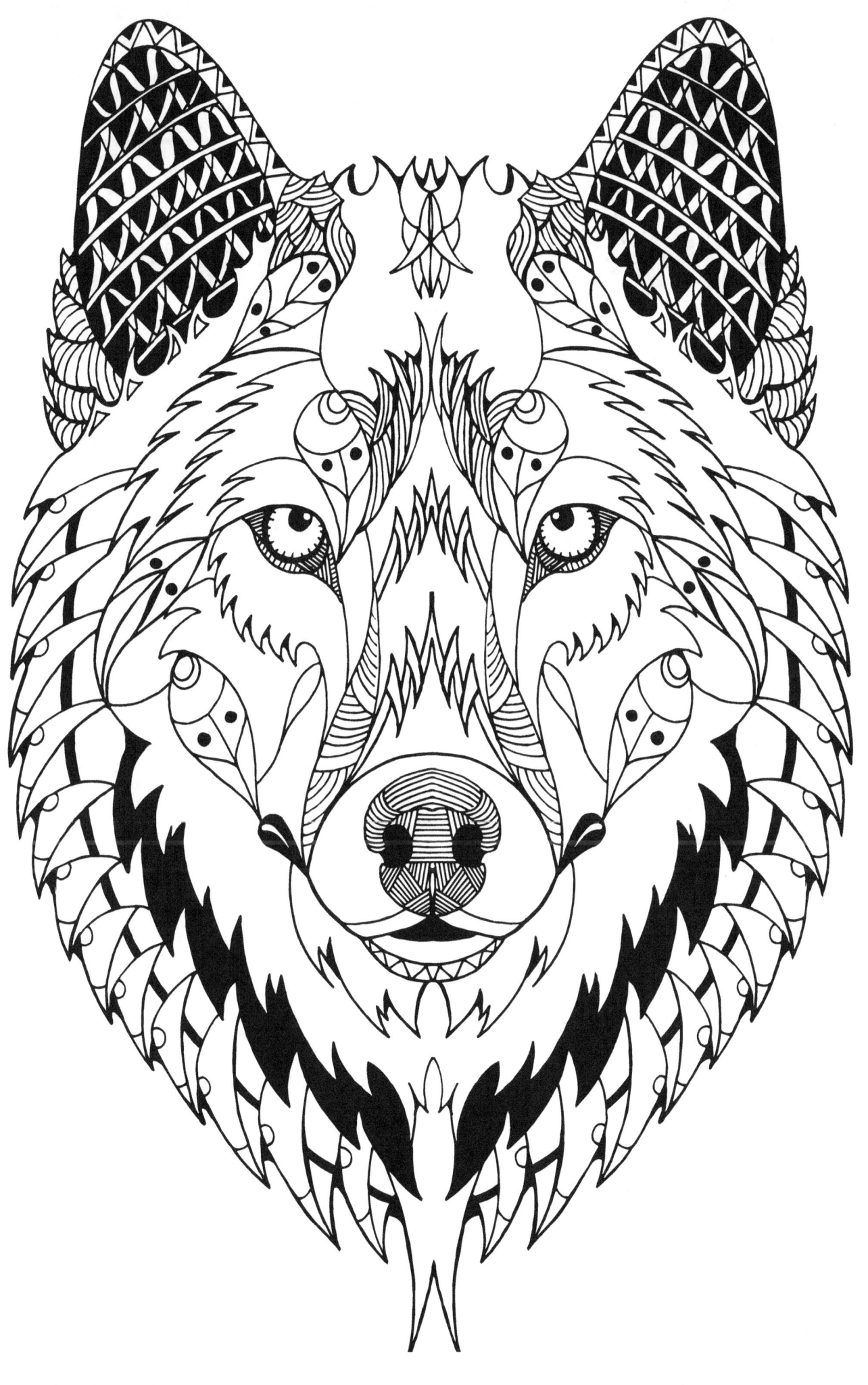

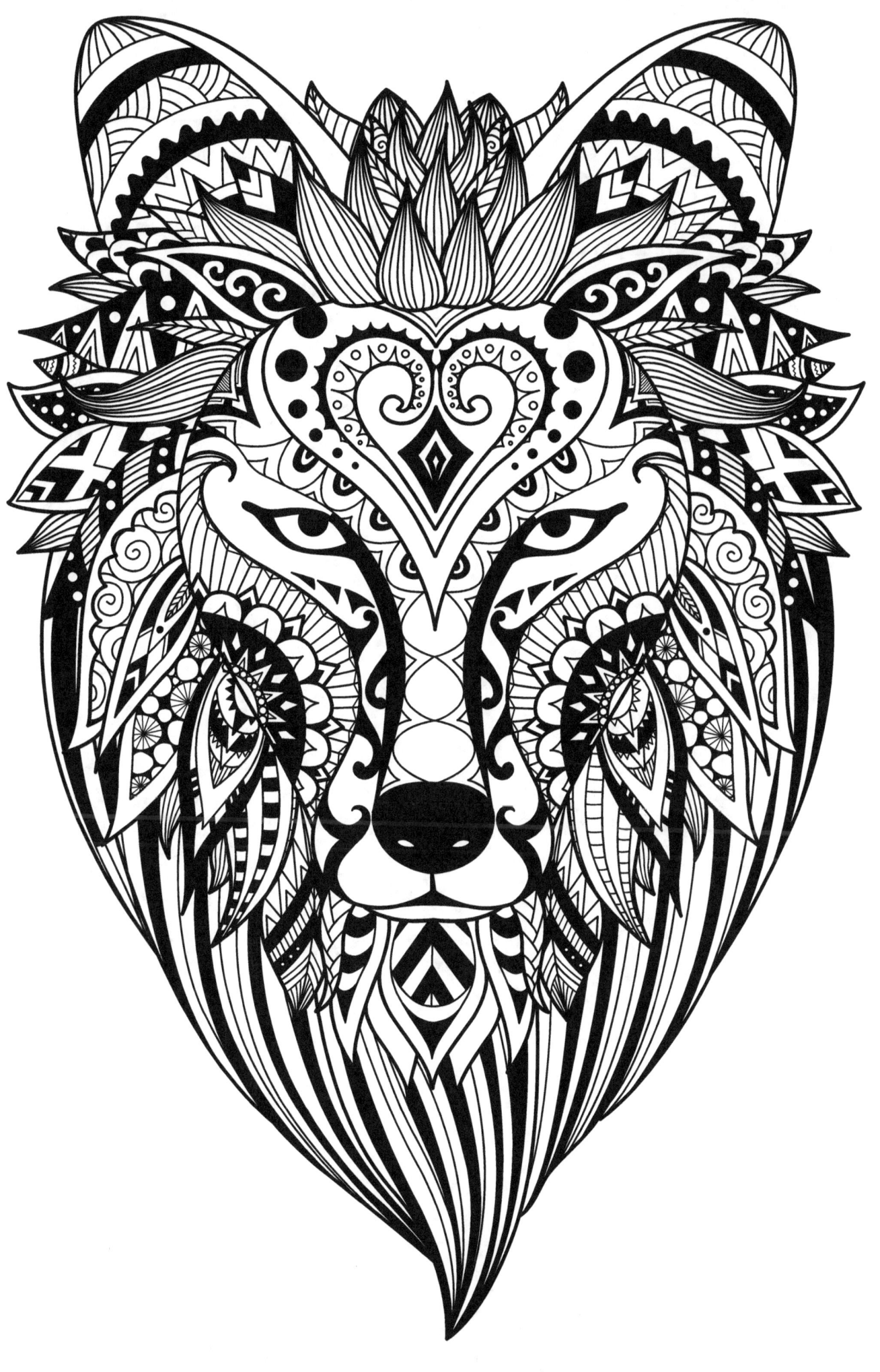

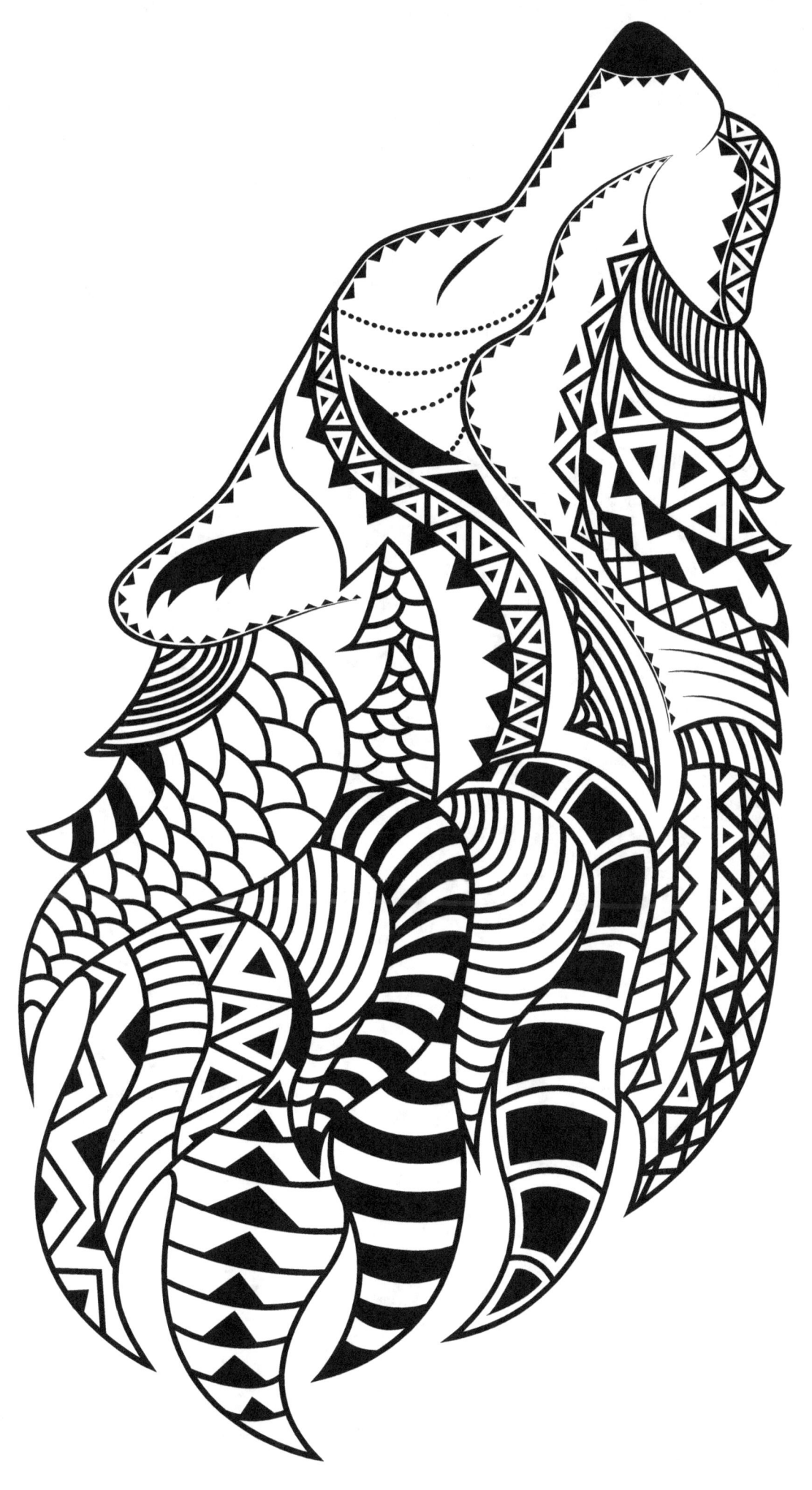

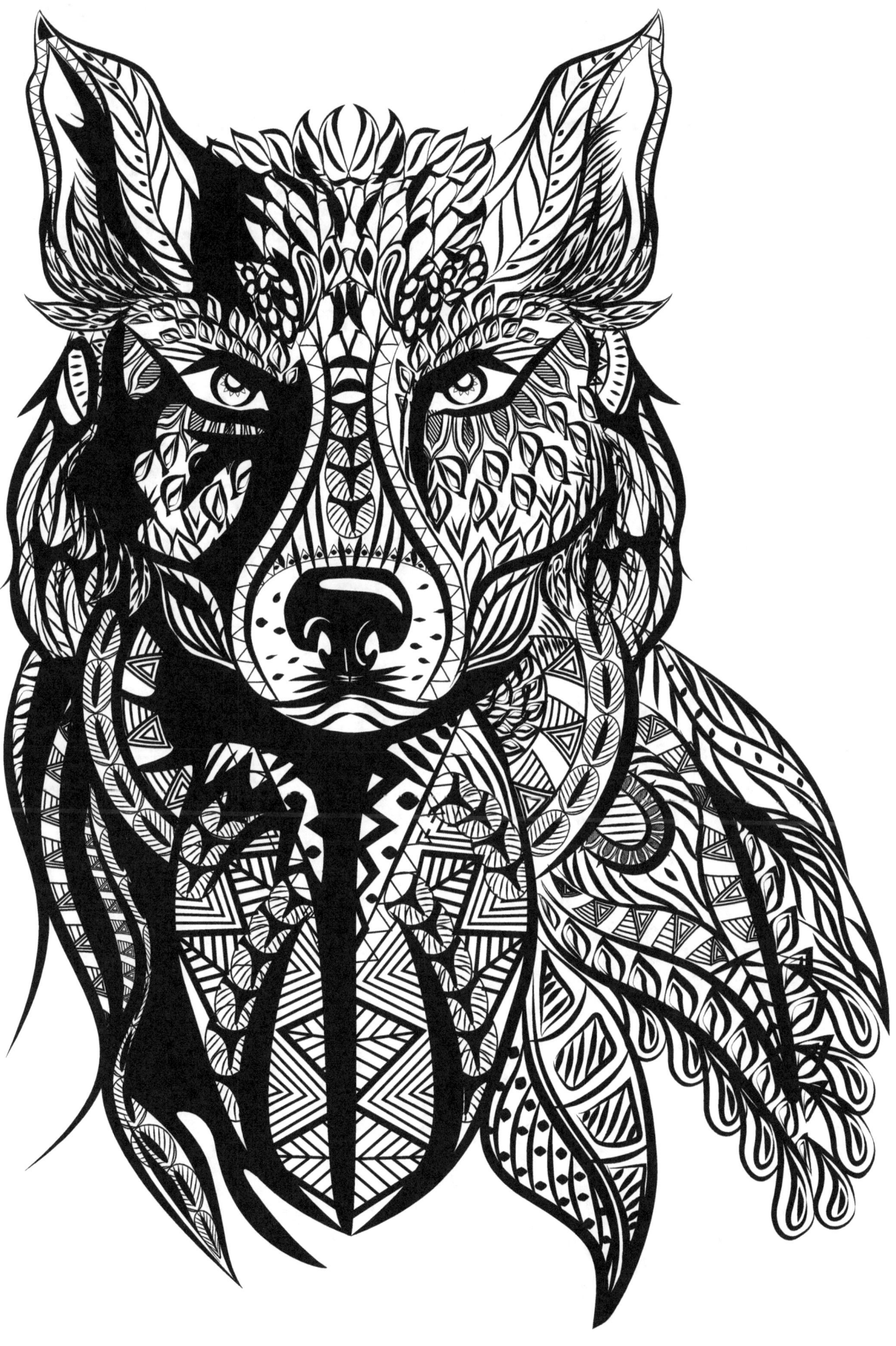

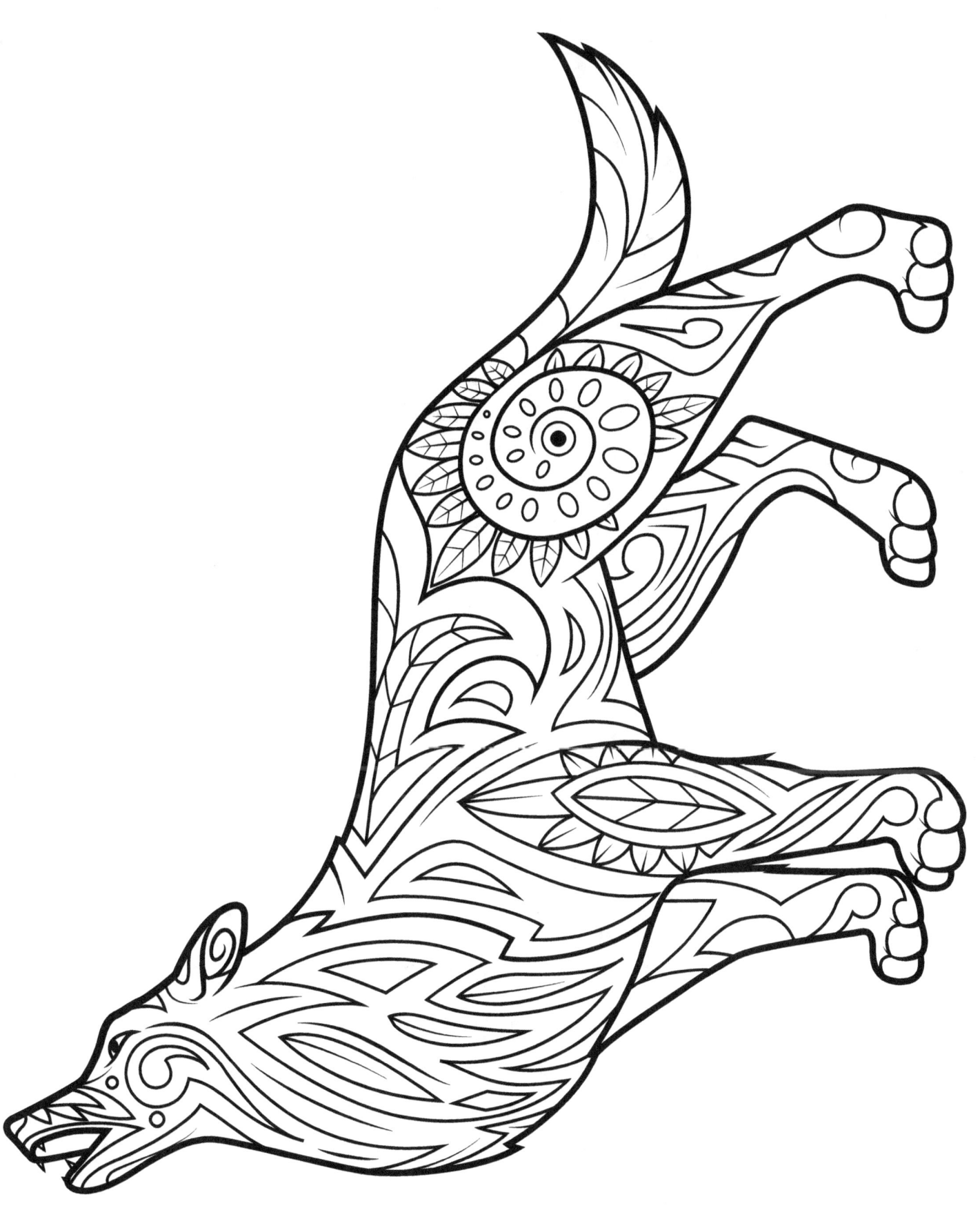

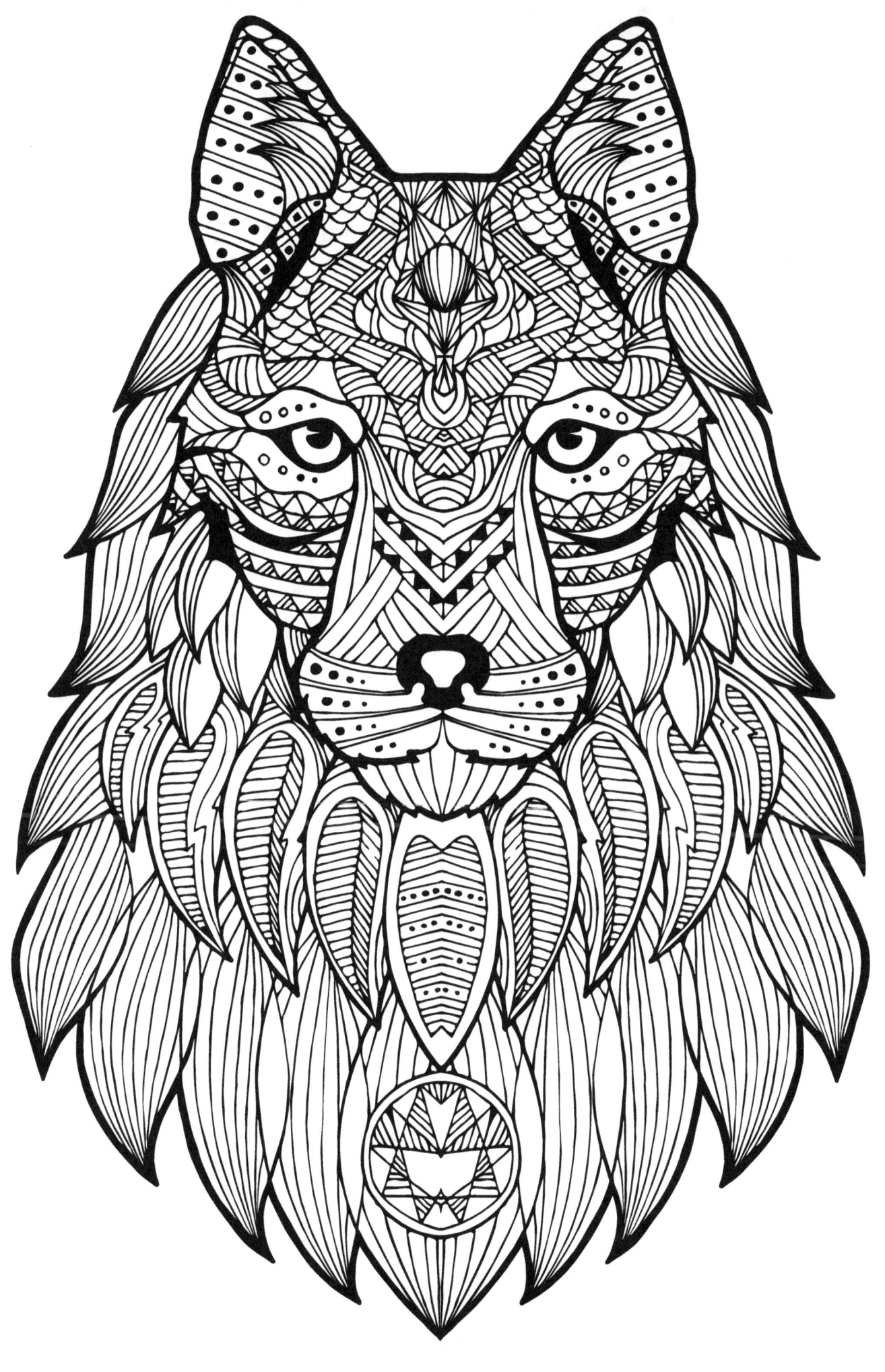

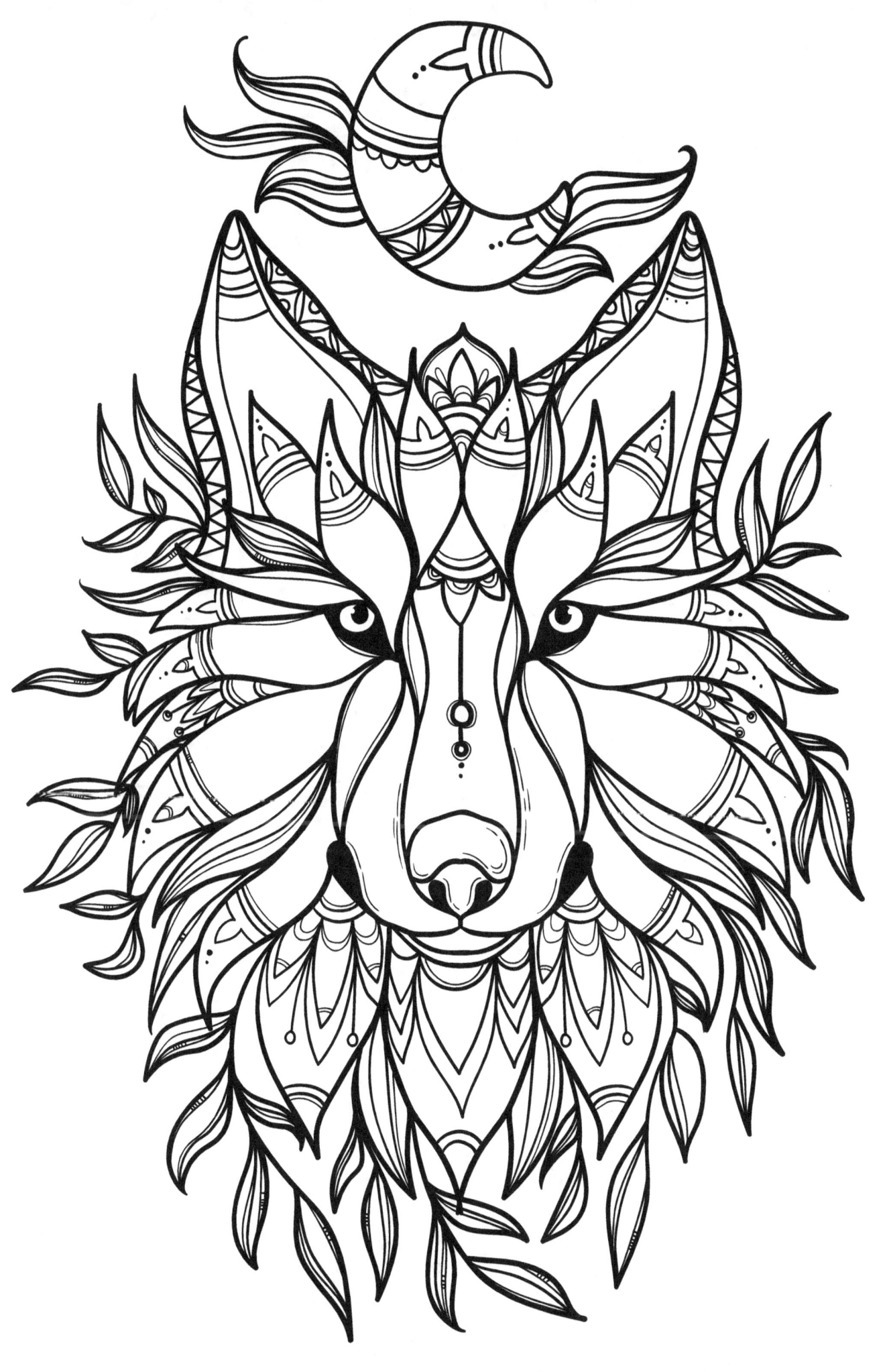

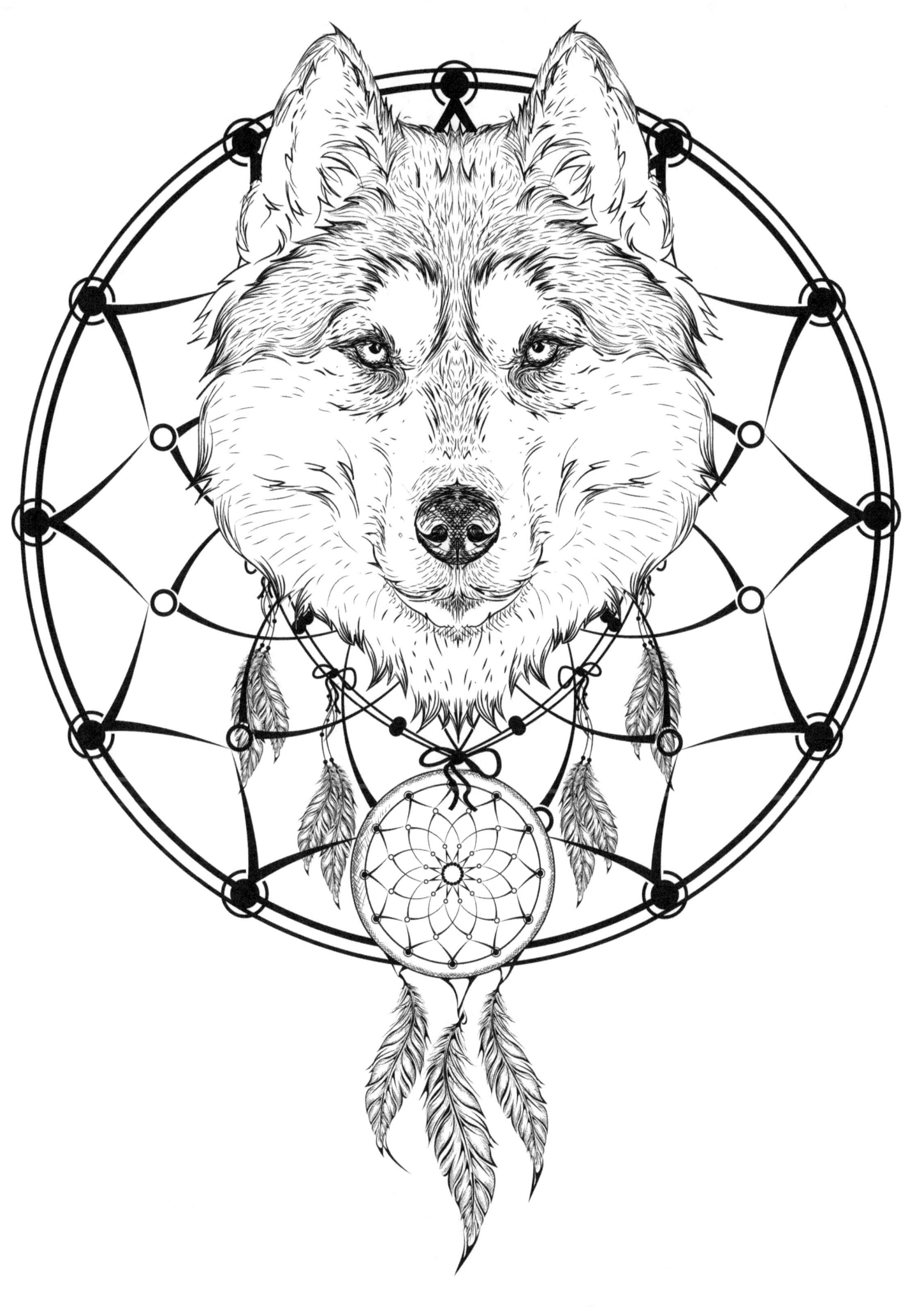

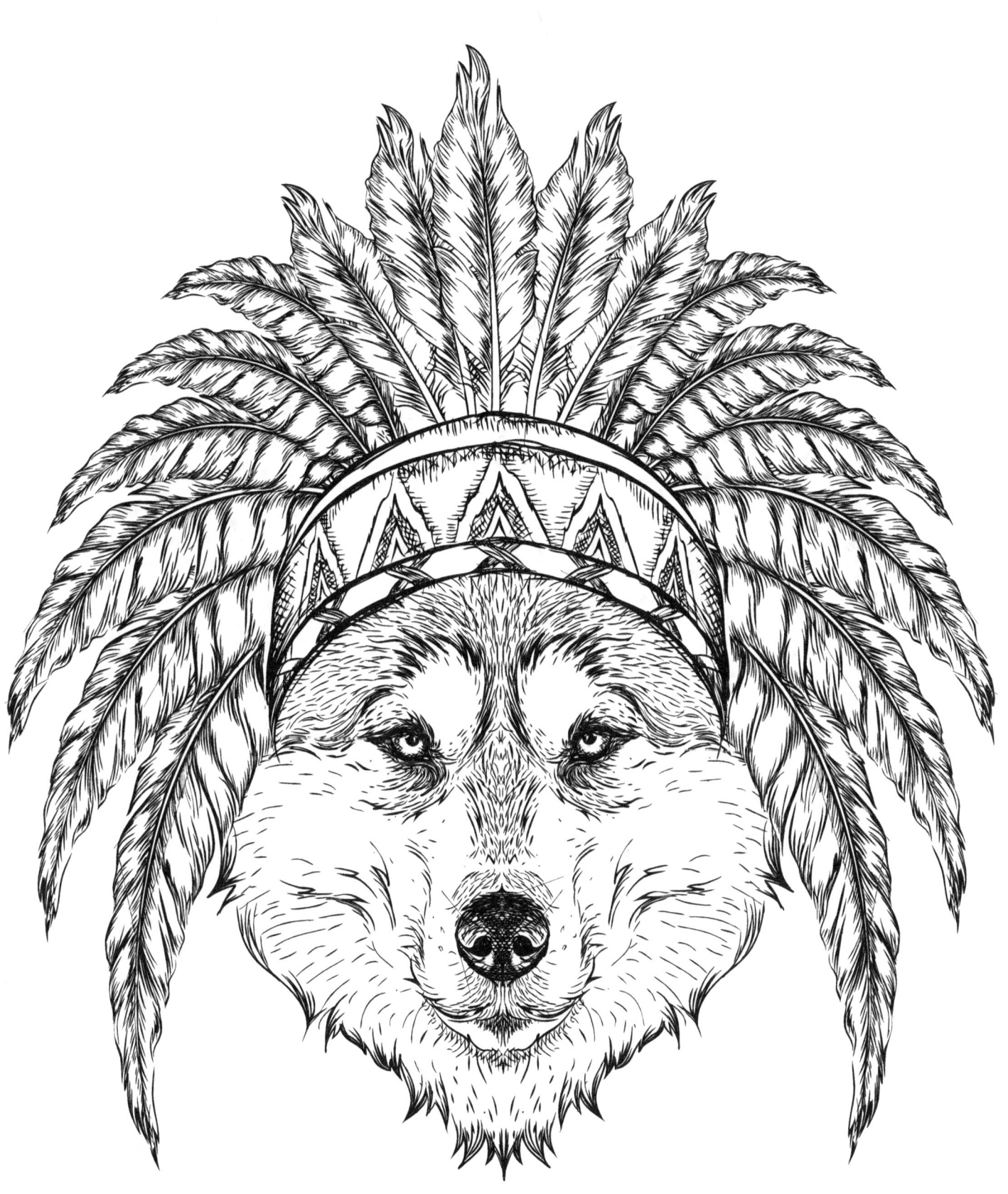

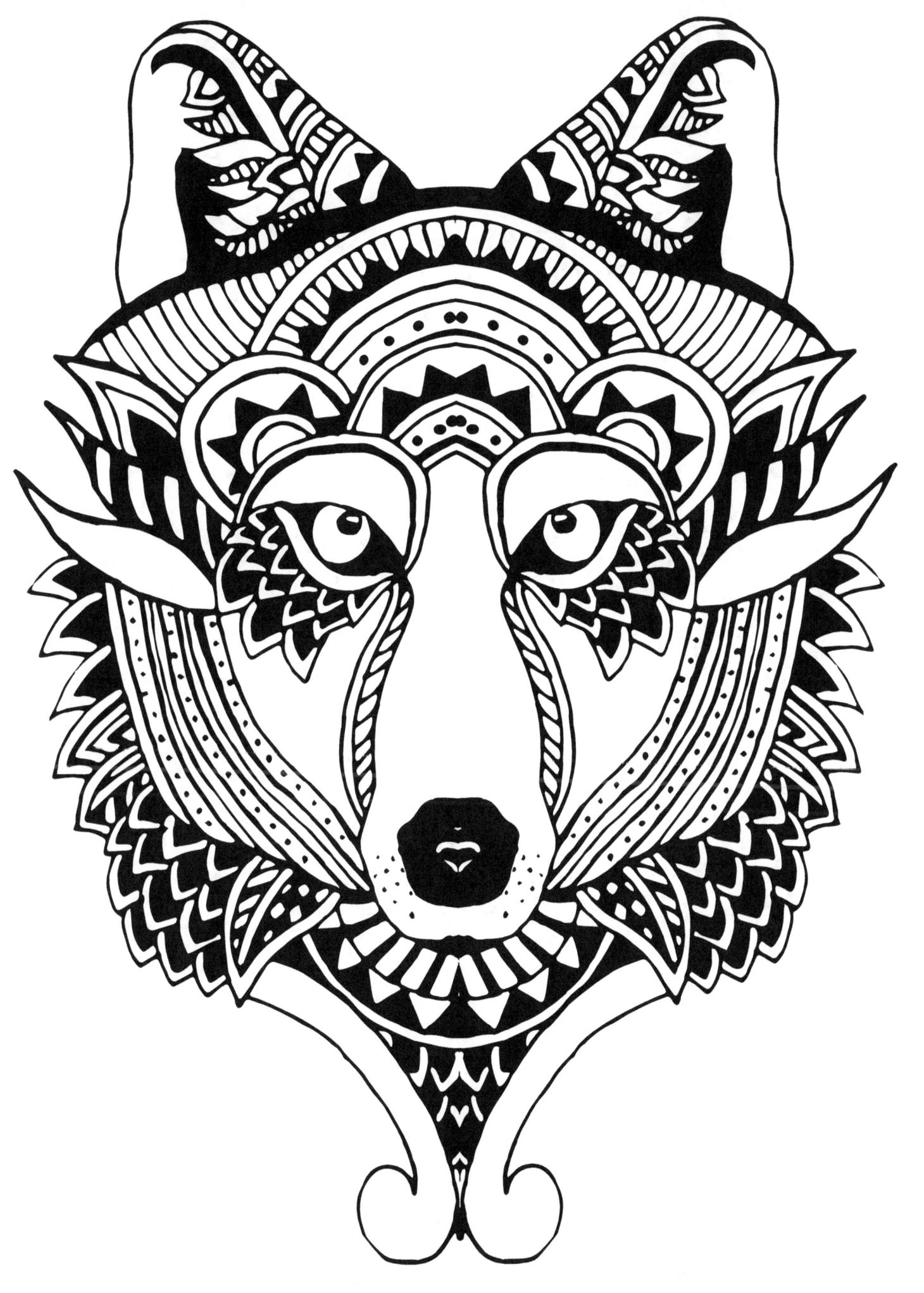

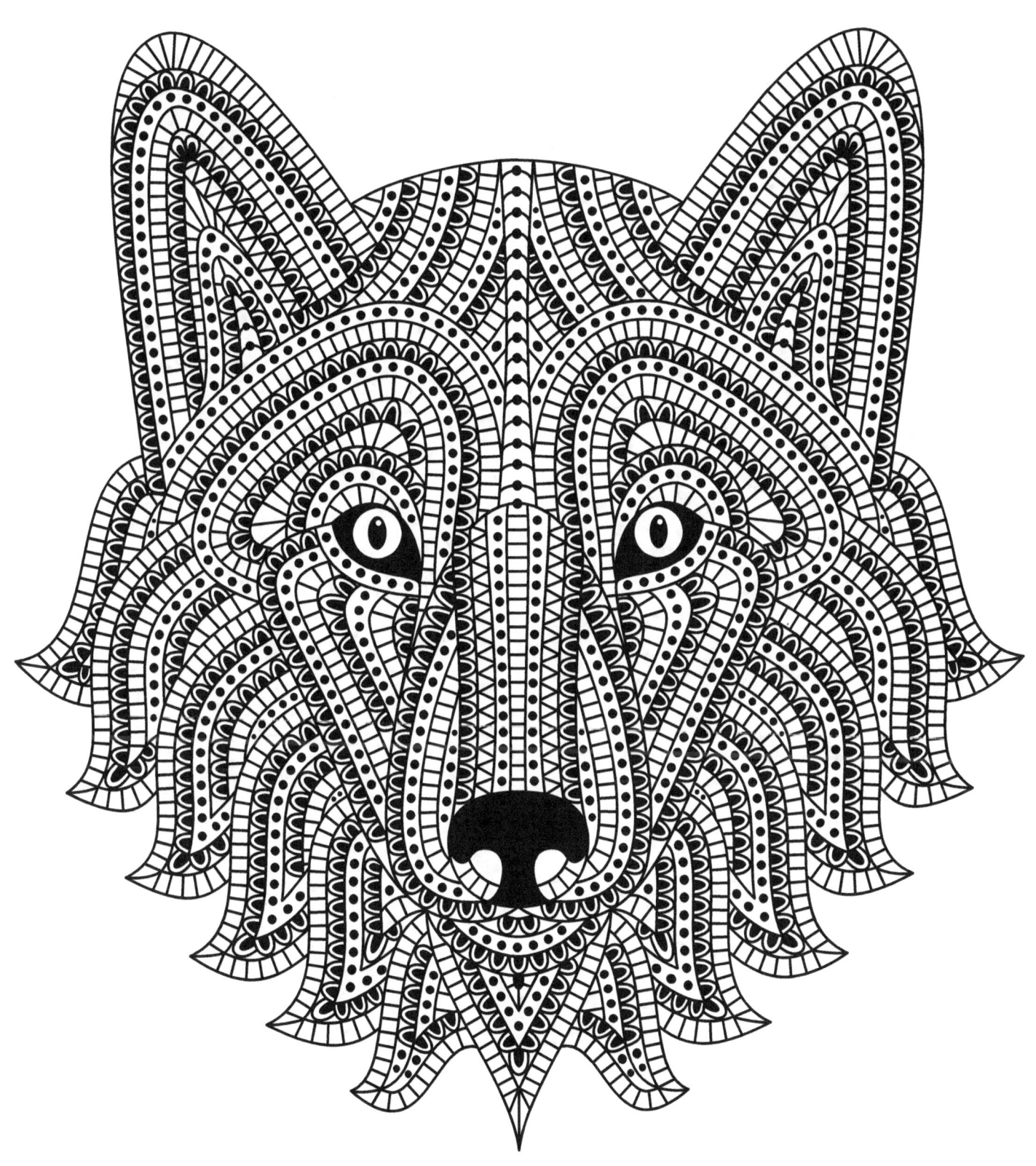

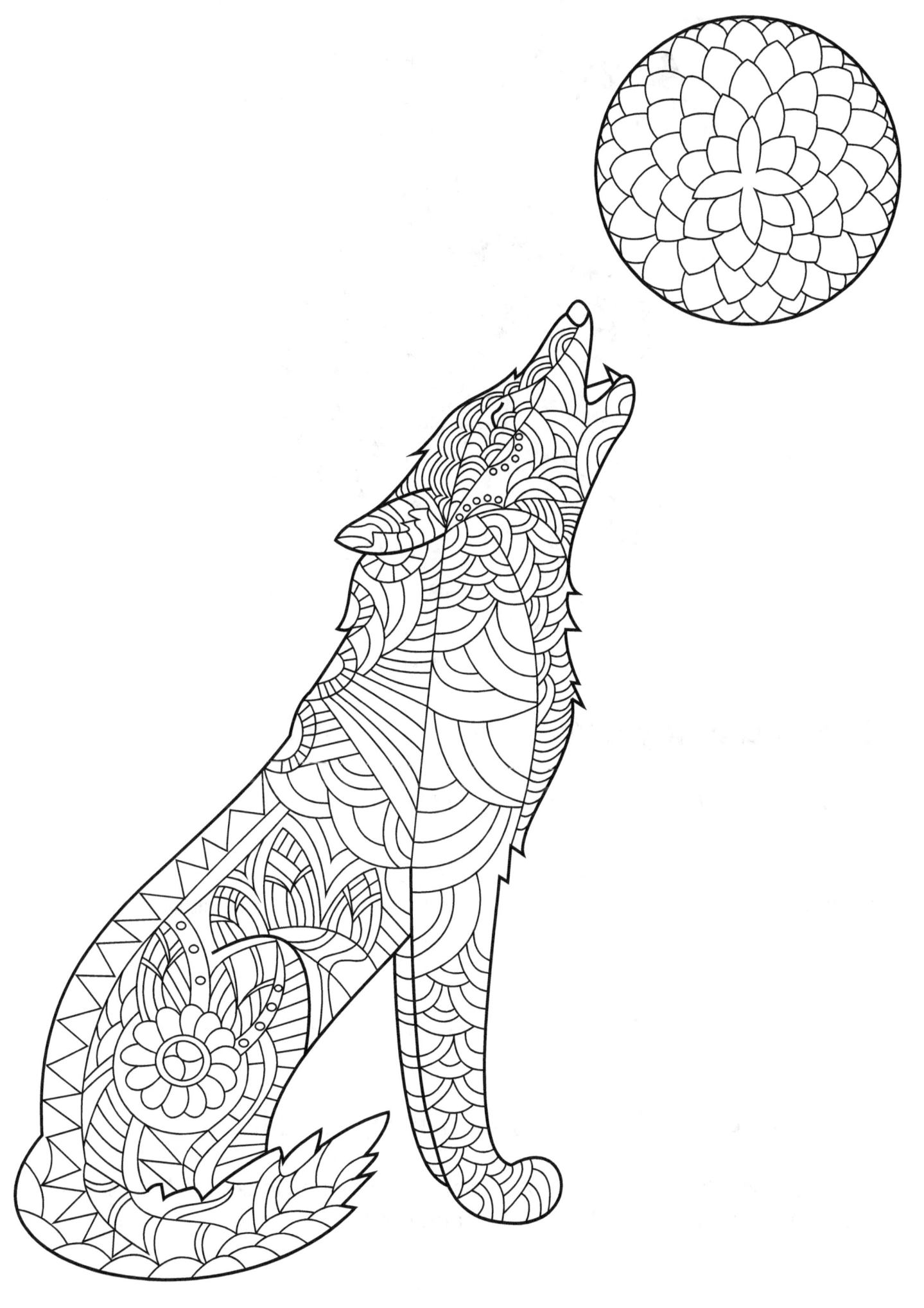

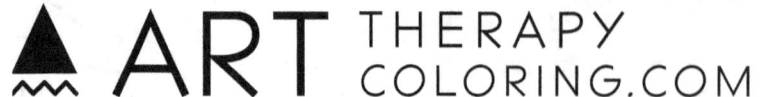

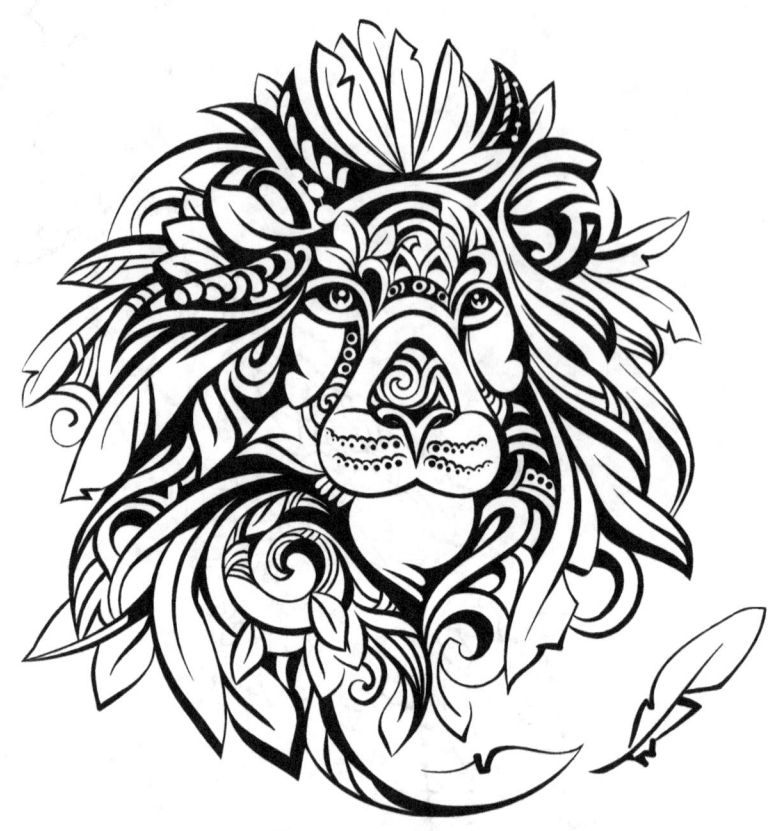

Did You Enjoy Our Coloring Book?

We Want To Hear About It!

Help spread the word about our coloring books! The best way to spread the word is through reviews. We know how busy you are, especially with all of that coloring, but we would appreciate it!

Visit our website at www.arttherapycoloring.com

Over 200 Art Therapy Coloring Books

See our collection of over 200 Art Therapy Coloring Books for Adults, Men, Women, Seniors, Teens, Kids, Boys, and Girls.

Coloring Books For Adults

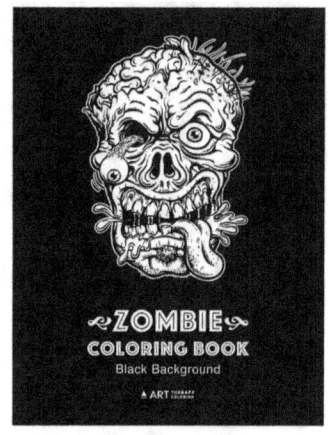

~ZOMBIE~
COLORING BOOK
Black Background

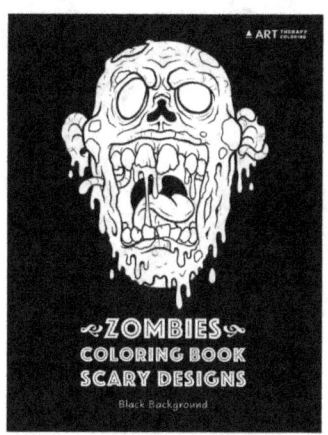

~ZOMBIES~
COLORING BOOK
SCARY DESIGNS
Black Background

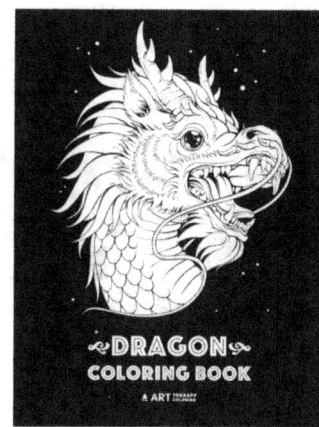

~DRAGON~
COLORING BOOK

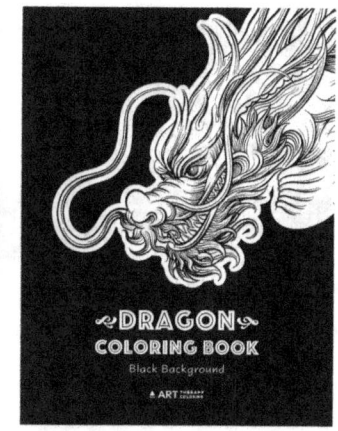

~DRAGON~
COLORING BOOK
Black Background

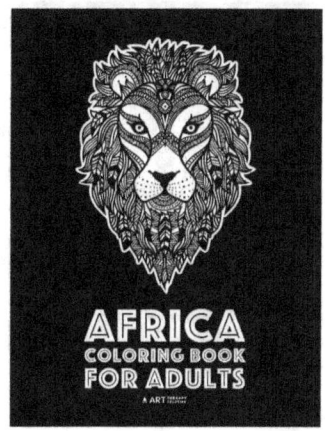

AFRICA
COLORING BOOK
FOR ADULTS

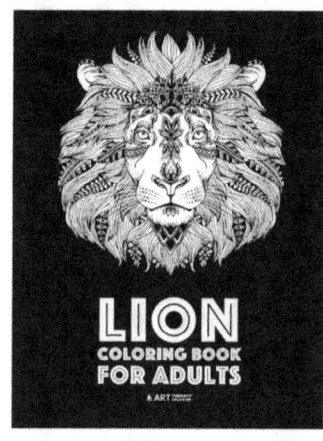

LION
COLORING BOOK
FOR ADULTS

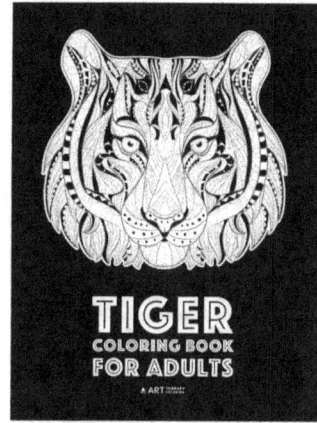

TIGER
COLORING BOOK
FOR ADULTS

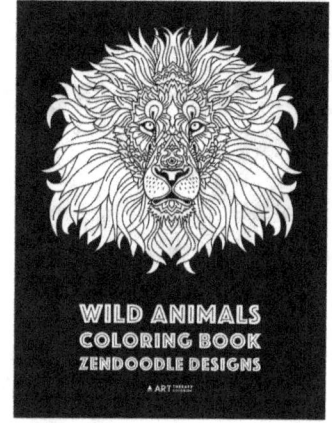

WILD ANIMALS
COLORING BOOK
ZENDOODLE DESIGNS

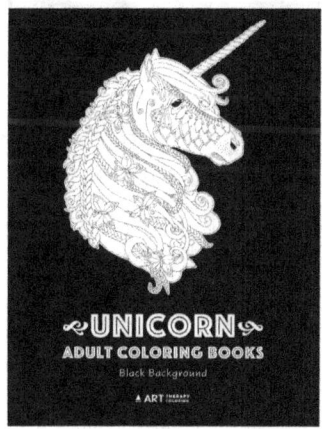

~UNICORN~
ADULT COLORING BOOKS
Black Background

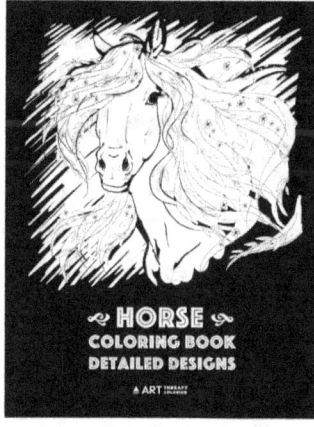

~HORSE~
COLORING BOOK
DETAILED DESIGNS

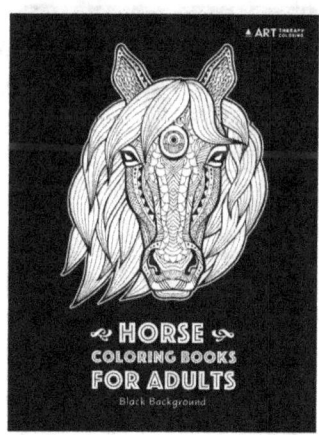

~HORSE~
COLORING BOOKS
FOR ADULTS
Black Background

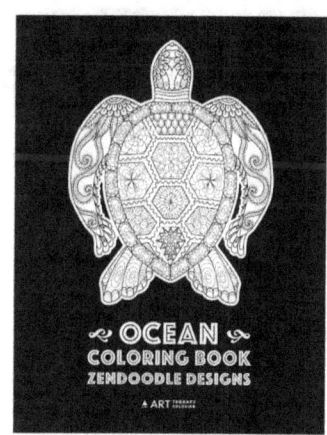

~OCEAN~
COLORING BOOK
ZENDOODLE DESIGNS

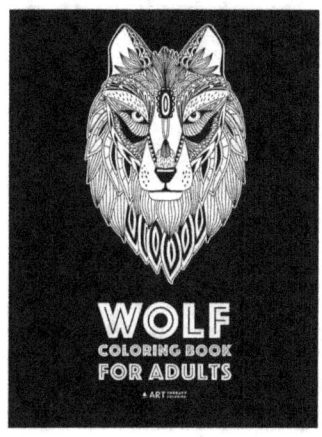

WOLF
COLORING BOOK
FOR ADULTS

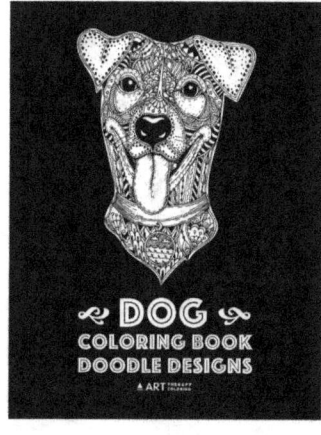

~DOG~
COLORING BOOK
DOODLE DESIGNS

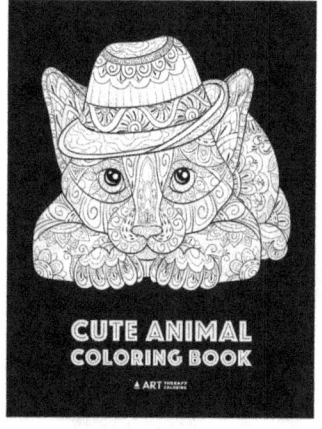

CUTE ANIMAL
COLORING BOOK

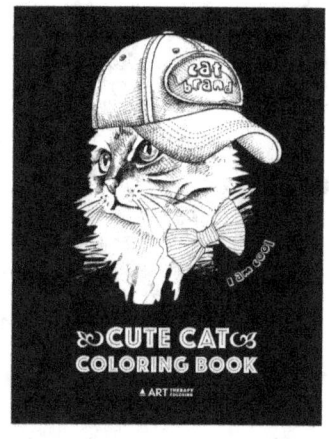

~CUTE CAT~
COLORING BOOK

Coloring Books For Adults

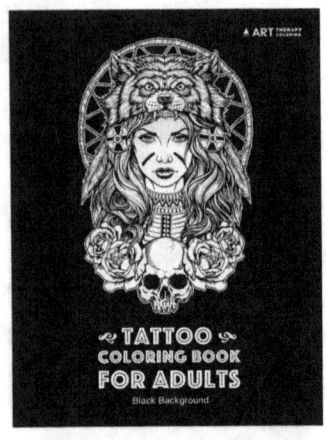

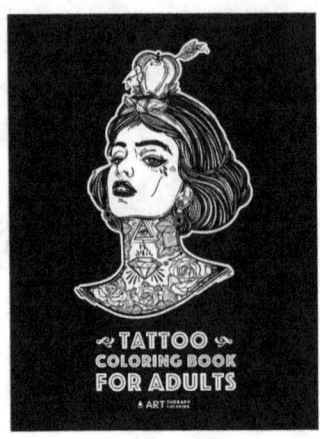

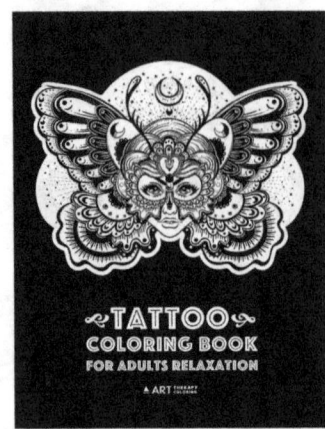

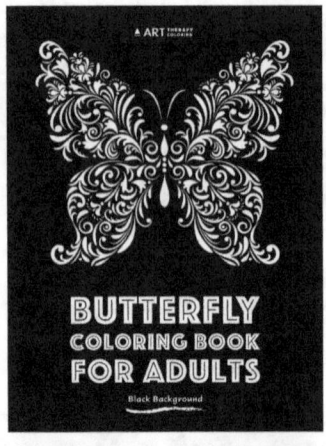

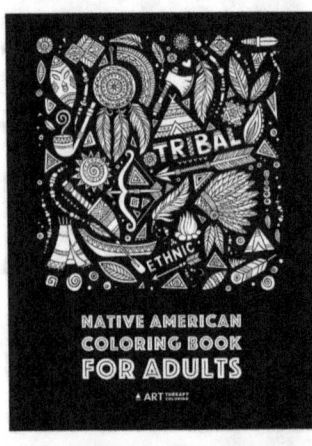

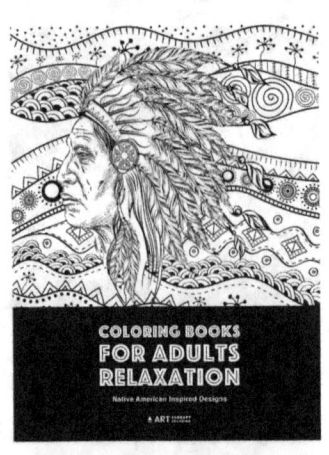

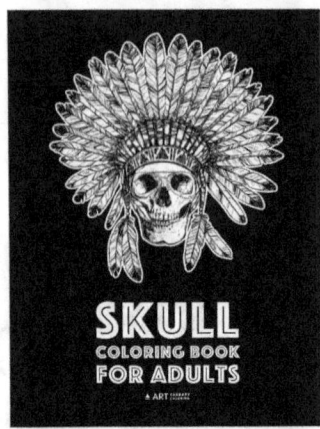

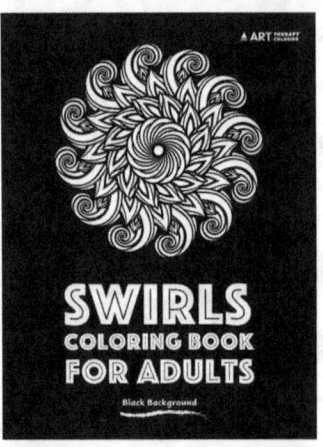

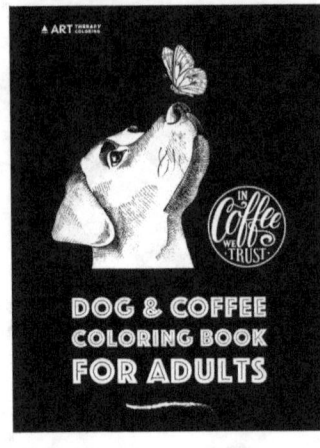

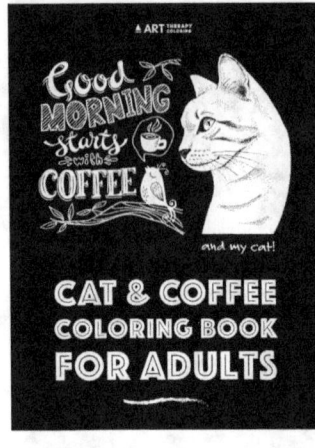

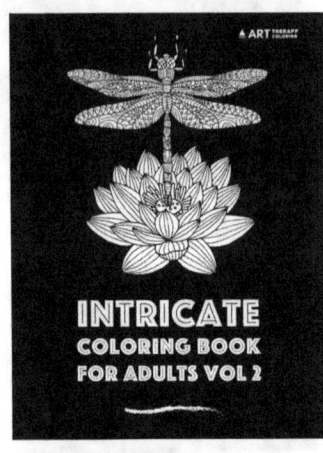

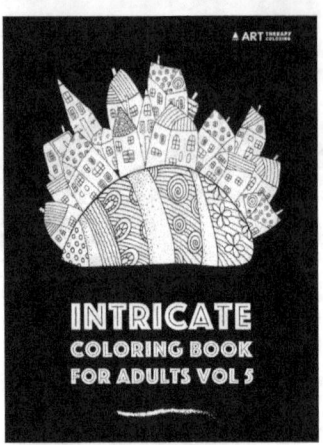

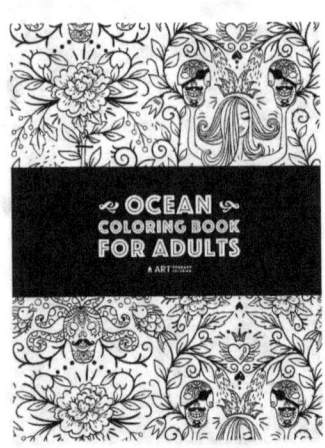

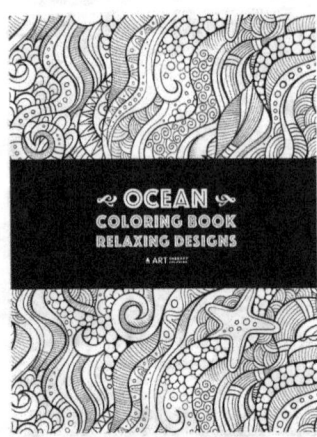

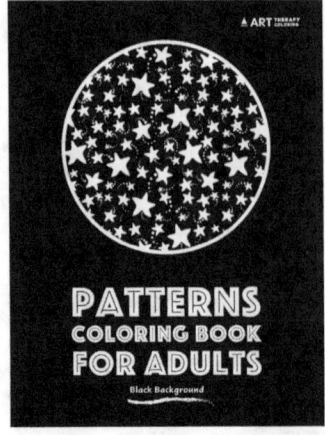

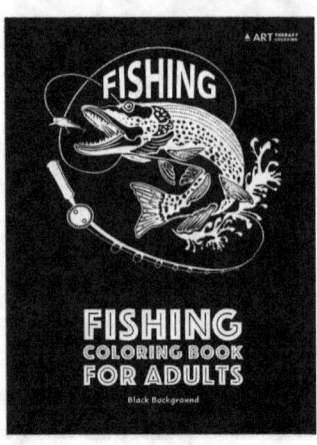

Coloring Books For Adults

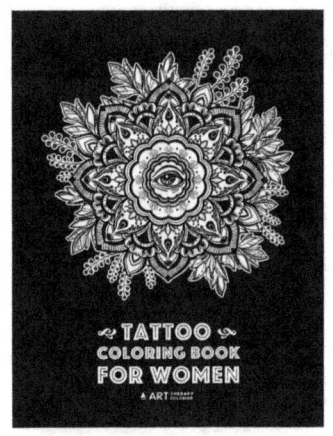

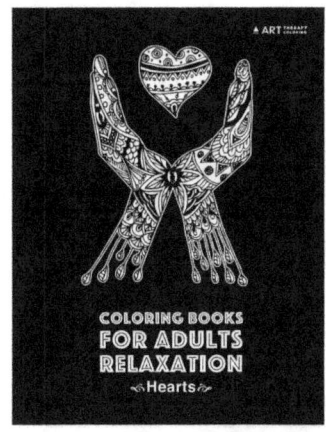

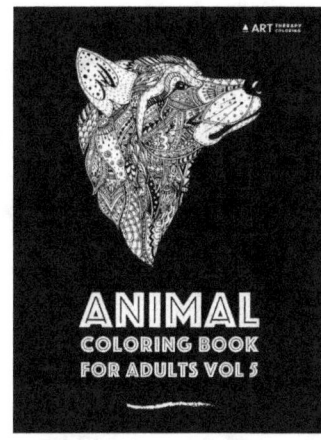

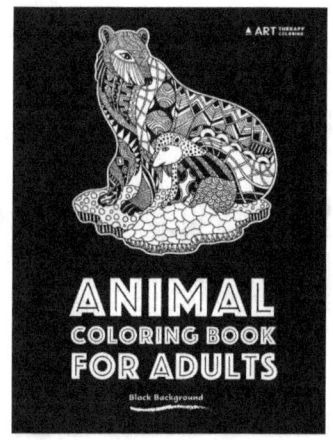

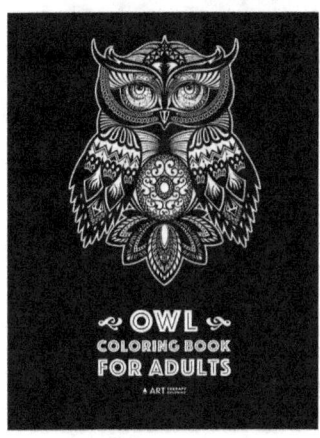

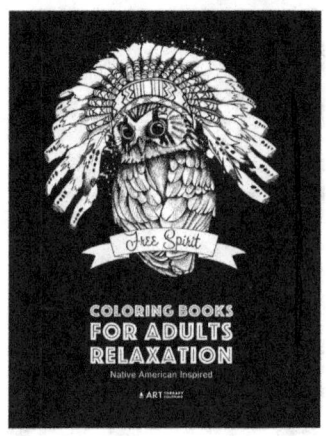

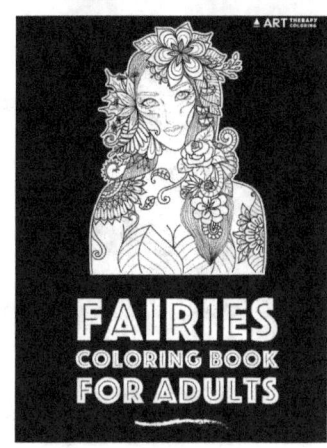

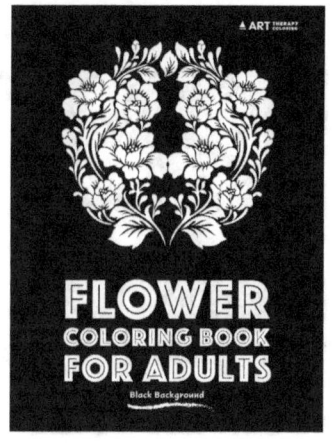

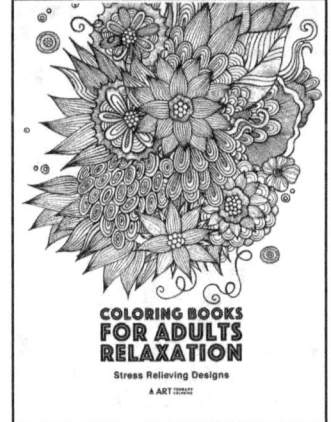

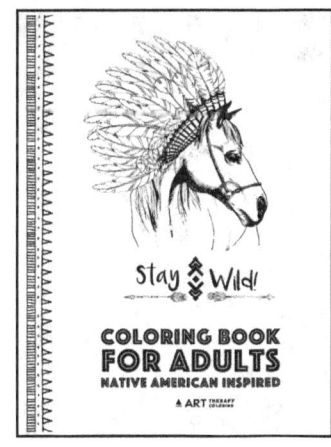

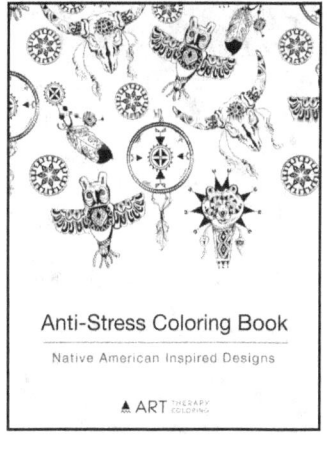

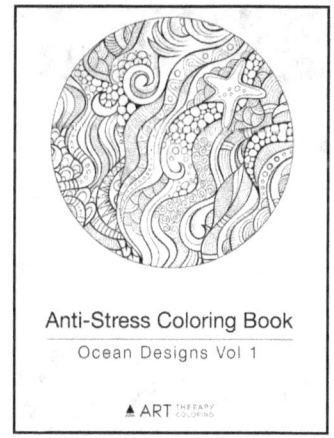

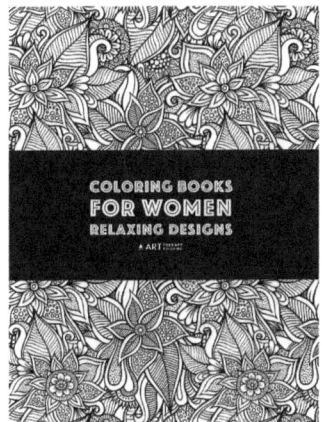

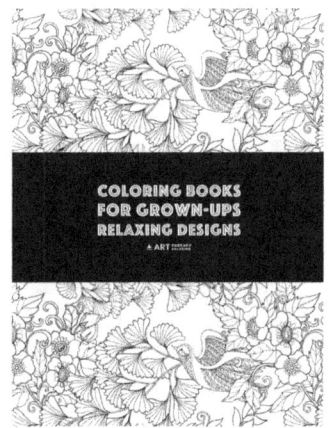

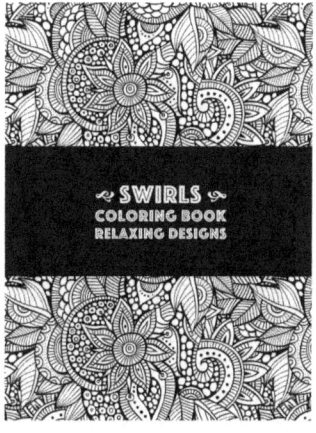

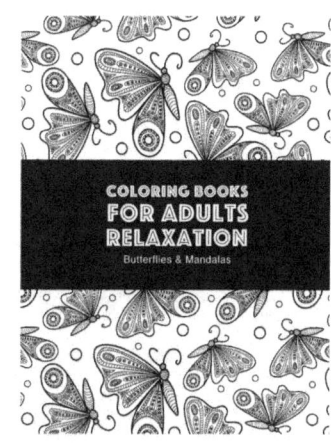

Coloring Books For Men

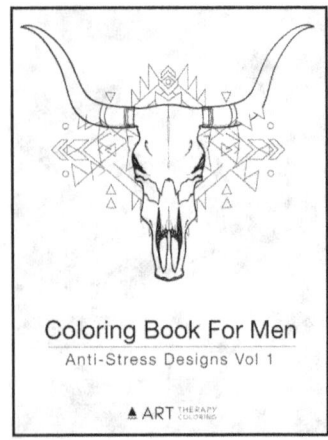

Coloring Book For Men
Anti-Stress Designs Vol 1

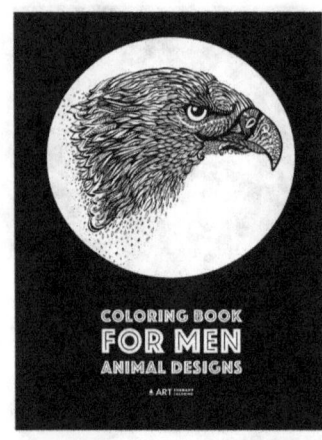

COLORING BOOK
FOR MEN
ANIMAL DESIGNS

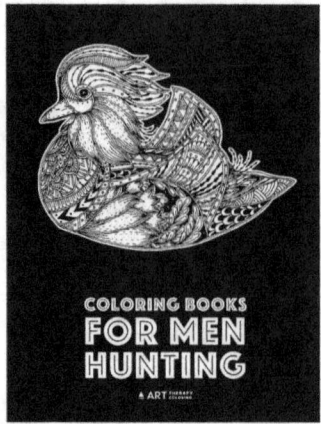

COLORING BOOKS
FOR MEN
HUNTING

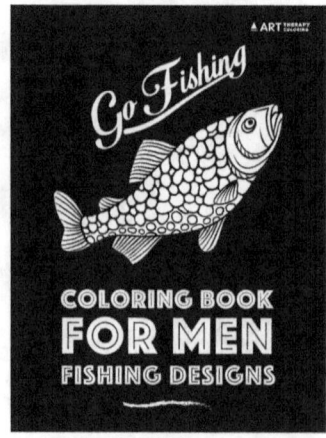

Go Fishing
COLORING BOOK
FOR MEN
FISHING DESIGNS

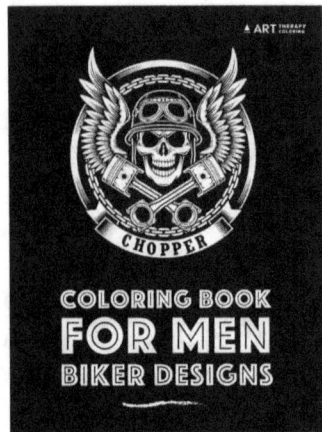

COLORING BOOK
FOR MEN
BIKER DESIGNS

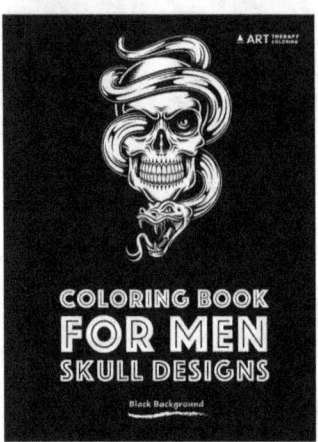

COLORING BOOK
FOR MEN
SKULL DESIGNS
Black Background

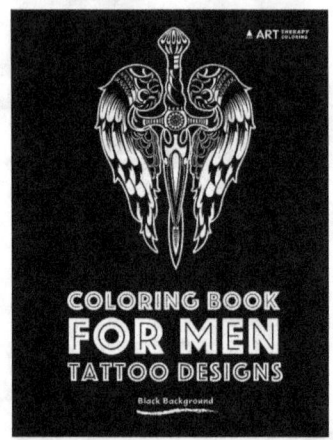

COLORING BOOK
FOR MEN
TATTOO DESIGNS
Black Background

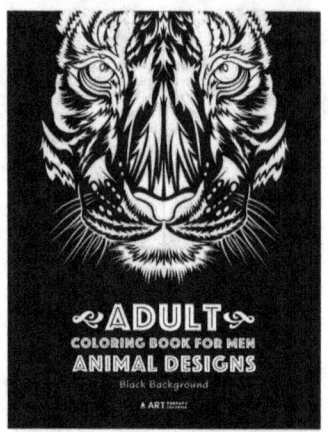

ADULT
COLORING BOOK FOR MEN
ANIMAL DESIGNS
Black Background

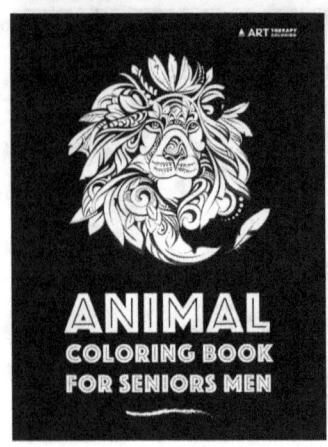

ANIMAL
COLORING BOOK
FOR SENIORS MEN

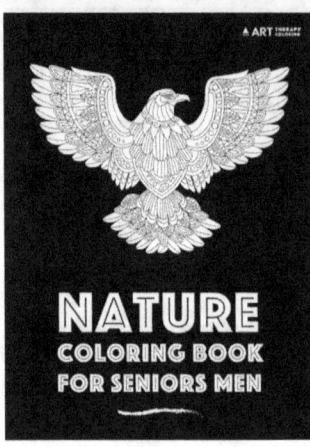

NATURE
COLORING BOOK
FOR SENIORS MEN

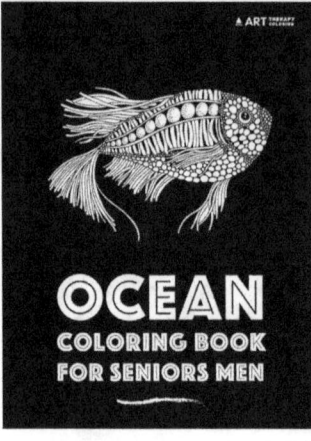

OCEAN
COLORING BOOK
FOR SENIORS MEN

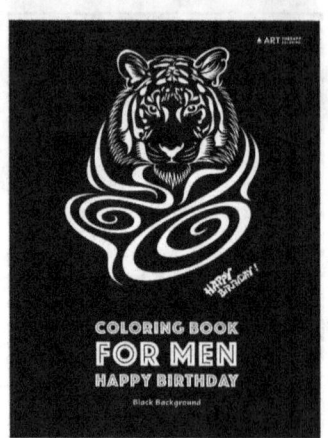

COLORING BOOK
FOR MEN
HAPPY BIRTHDAY
Black Background

Coloring Books For Seniors

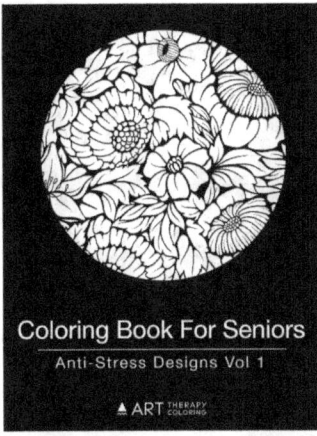

Coloring Book For Seniors
Anti-Stress Designs Vol 1

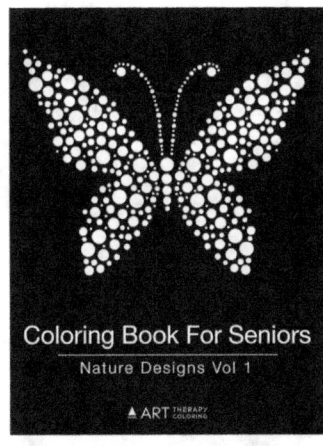

Coloring Book For Seniors
Nature Designs Vol 1

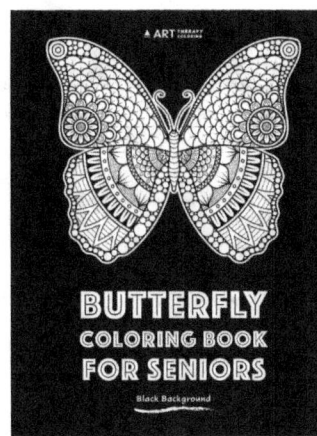

BUTTERFLY
COLORING BOOK
FOR SENIORS
Black Background

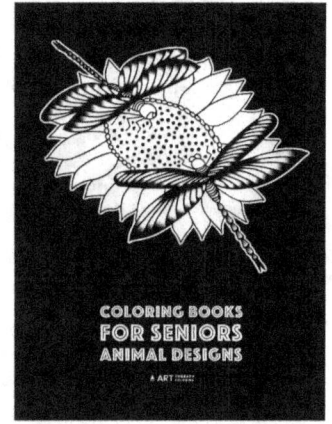

COLORING BOOKS
FOR SENIORS
ANIMAL DESIGNS

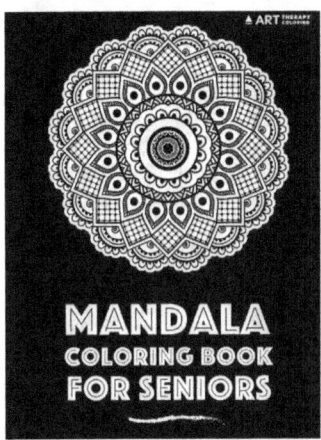

MANDALA
COLORING BOOK
FOR SENIORS

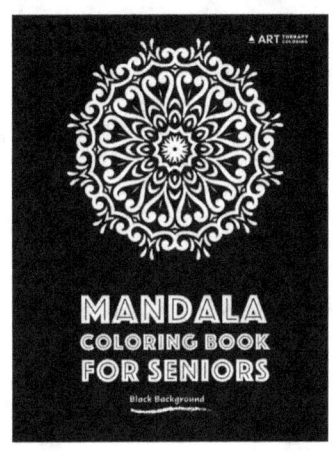

MANDALA
COLORING BOOK
FOR SENIORS
Black Background

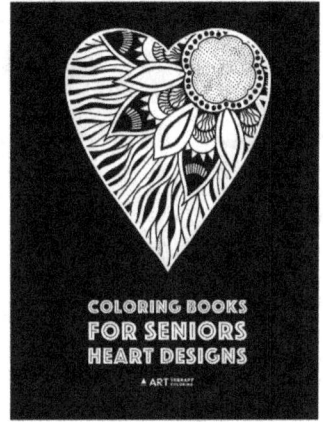

COLORING BOOKS
FOR SENIORS
HEART DESIGNS

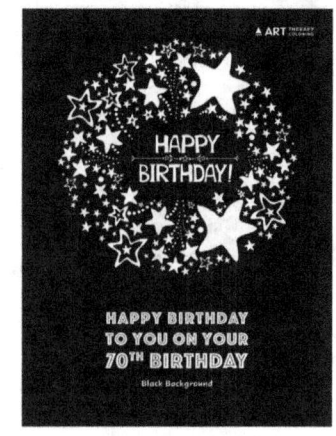

HAPPY BIRTHDAY
TO YOU ON YOUR
70TH BIRTHDAY
Black Background

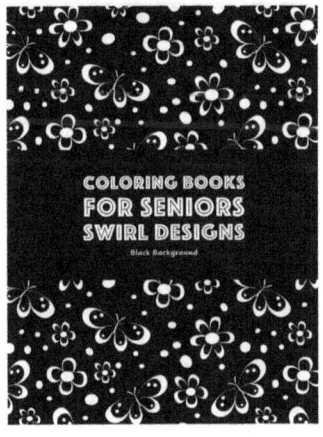

COLORING BOOKS
FOR SENIORS
SWIRL DESIGNS
Black Background

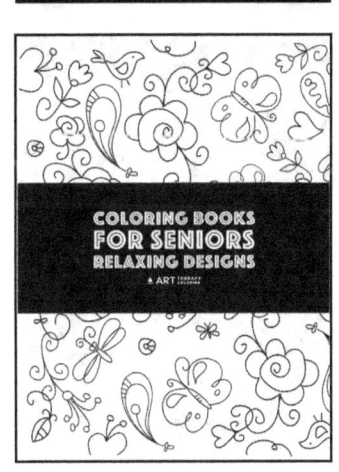

COLORING BOOKS
FOR SENIORS
RELAXING DESIGNS

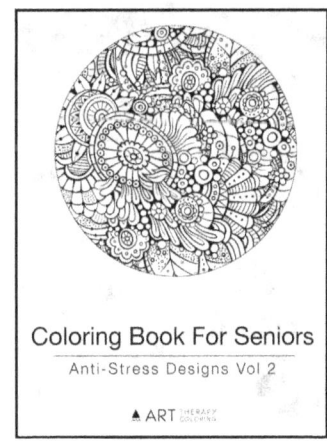

Coloring Book For Seniors
Anti-Stress Designs Vol 2

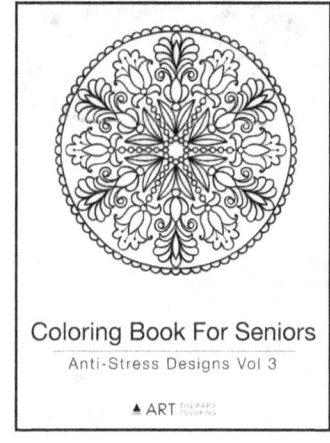

Coloring Book For Seniors
Anti-Stress Designs Vol 3

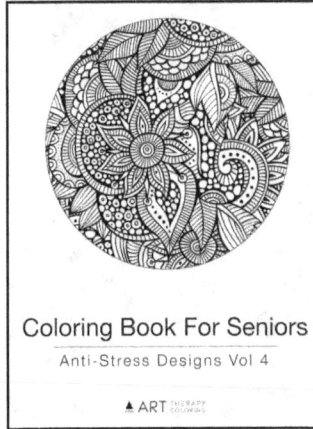

Coloring Book For Seniors
Anti-Stress Designs Vol 4

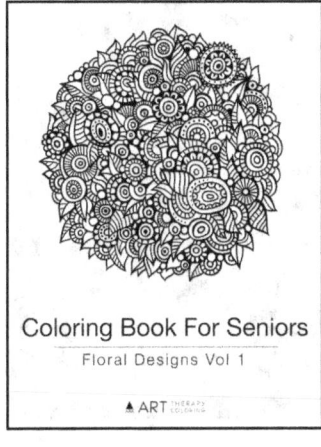

Coloring Book For Seniors
Floral Designs Vol 1

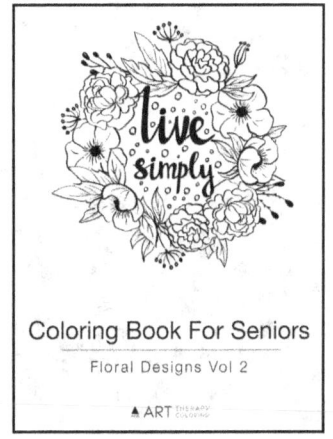

Coloring Book For Seniors
Floral Designs Vol 2

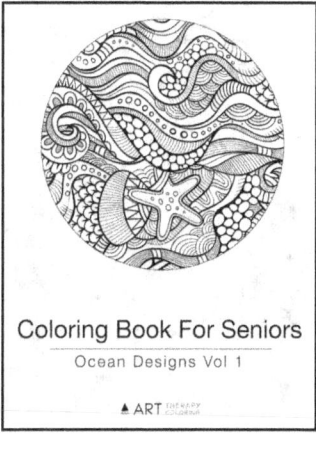

Coloring Book For Seniors
Ocean Designs Vol 1

Coloring Books For Teens

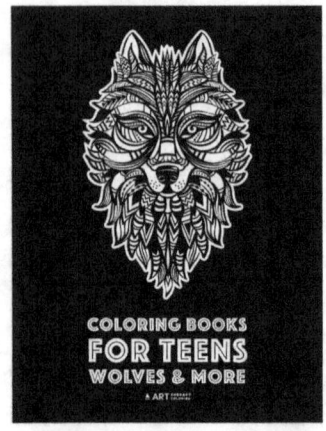

COLORING BOOKS FOR TEENS WOLVES & MORE

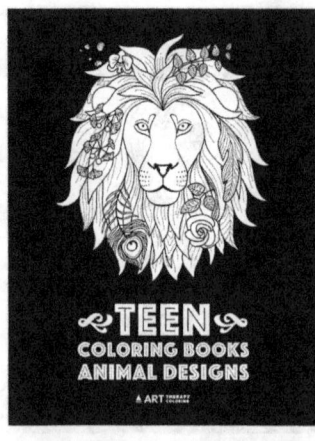

TEEN COLORING BOOKS ANIMAL DESIGNS

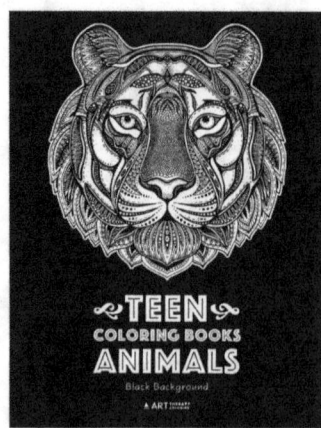

TEEN COLORING BOOKS ANIMALS — Black Background

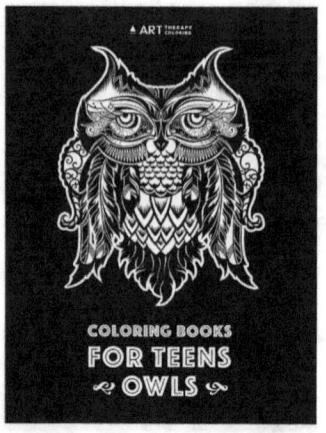

COLORING BOOKS FOR TEENS OWLS

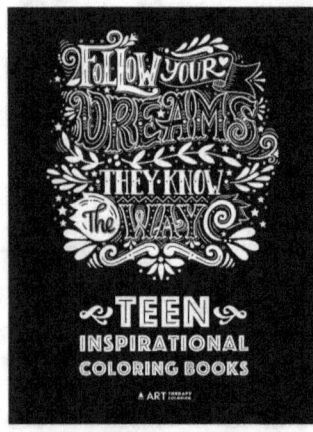

TEEN INSPIRATIONAL COLORING BOOKS

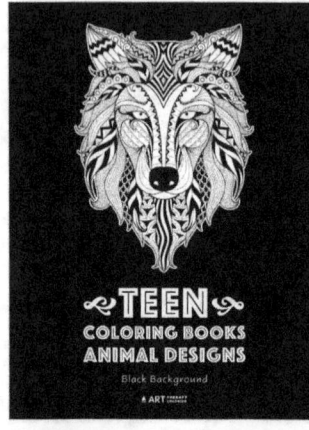

TEEN COLORING BOOKS ANIMAL DESIGNS — Black Background

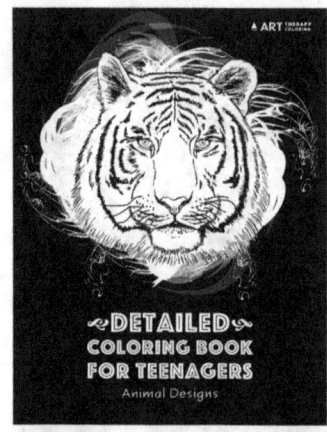

DETAILED COLORING BOOK FOR TEENAGERS — Animal Designs

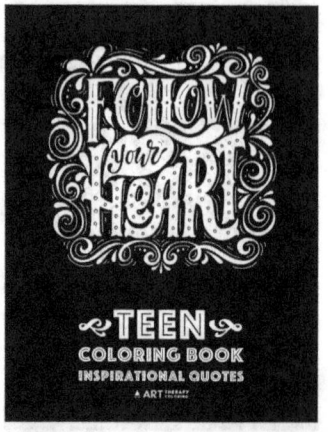

TEEN COLORING BOOK INSPIRATIONAL QUOTES

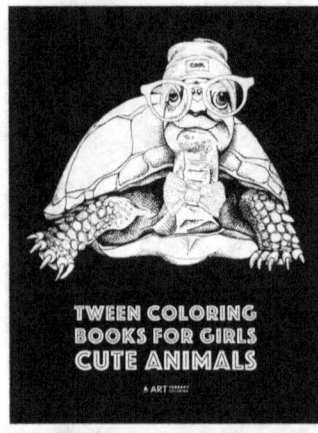

TWEEN COLORING BOOKS FOR GIRLS CUTE ANIMALS

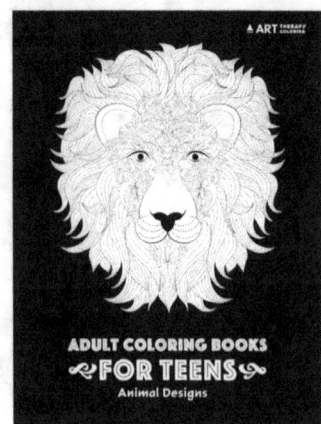

ADULT COLORING BOOKS FOR TEENS — Animal Designs

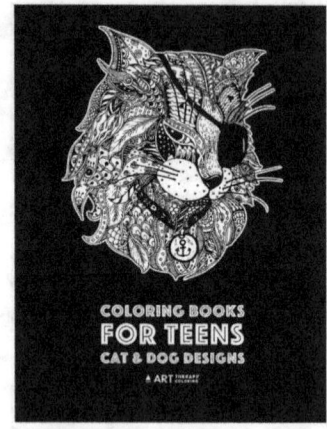

COLORING BOOKS FOR TEENS CAT & DOG DESIGNS

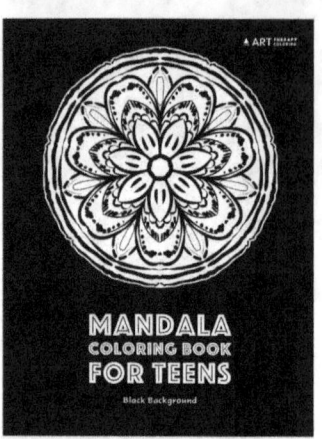

MANDALA COLORING BOOK FOR TEENS — Black Background

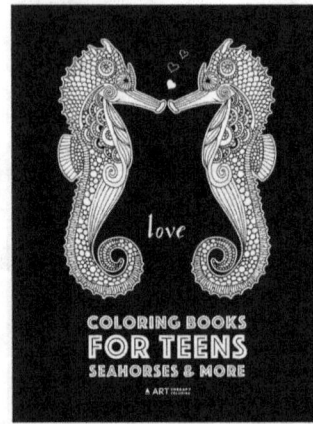

COLORING BOOKS FOR TEENS SEAHORSES & MORE

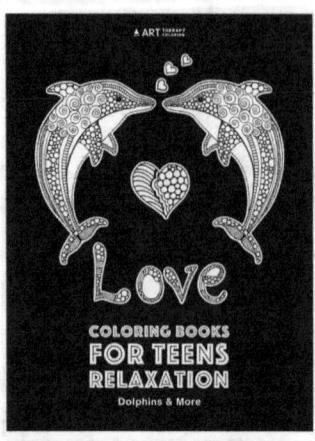

COLORING BOOKS FOR TEENS RELAXATION — Dolphins & More

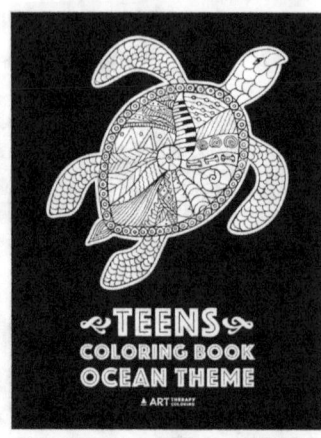

TEENS COLORING BOOK OCEAN THEME

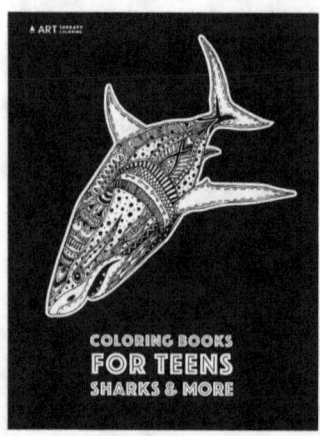

COLORING BOOKS FOR TEENS SHARKS & MORE

Coloring Books For Teens

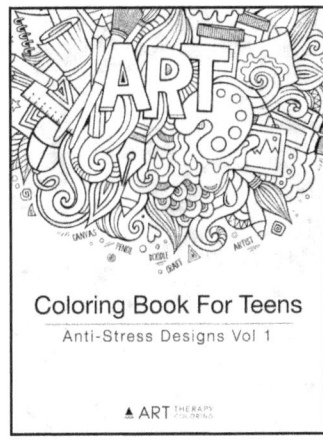

Coloring Book For Teens

Anti-Stress Designs Vol 1

▲ ART THERAPY COLORING

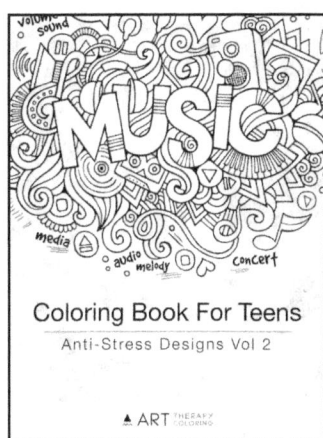

Coloring Book For Teens

Anti-Stress Designs Vol 2

▲ ART THERAPY COLORING

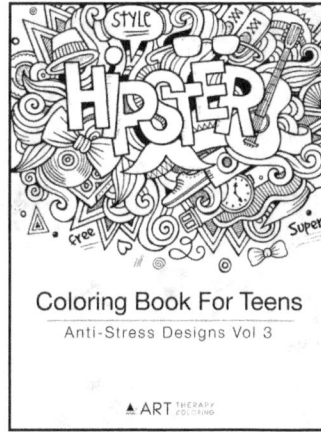

Coloring Book For Teens

Anti-Stress Designs Vol 3

▲ ART THERAPY COLORING

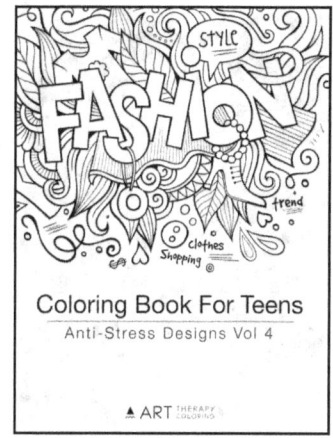

Coloring Book For Teens

Anti-Stress Designs Vol 4

▲ ART THERAPY COLORING

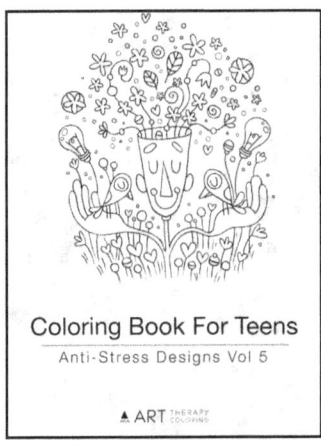

Coloring Book For Teens

Anti-Stress Designs Vol 5

▲ ART THERAPY COLORING

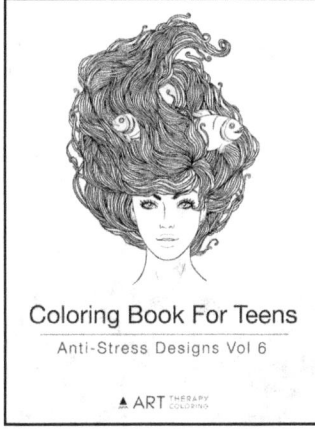

Coloring Book For Teens

Anti-Stress Designs Vol 6

▲ ART THERAPY COLORING

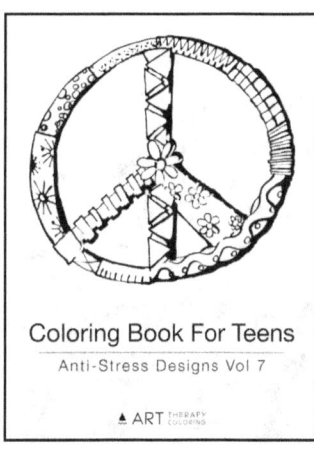

Coloring Book For Teens

Anti-Stress Designs Vol 7

▲ ART THERAPY COLORING

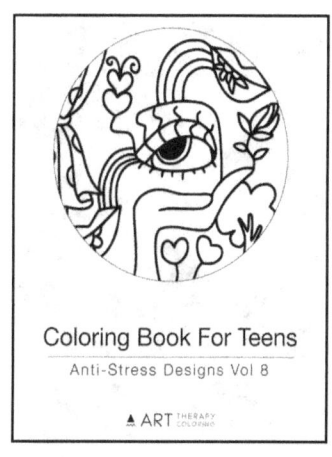

Coloring Book For Teens

Anti-Stress Designs Vol 8

▲ ART THERAPY COLORING

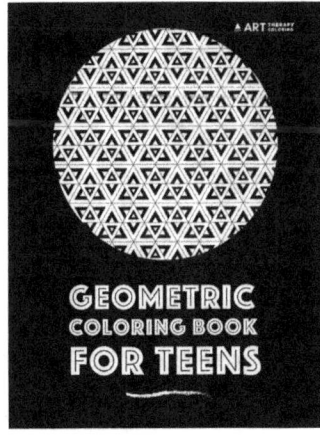

GEOMETRIC COLORING BOOK FOR TEENS

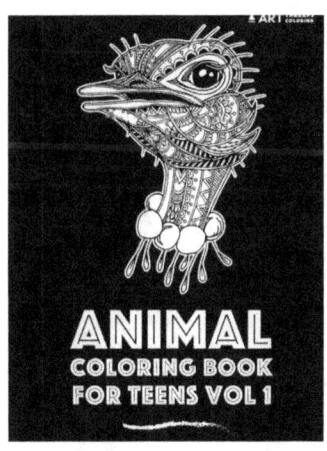

ANIMAL COLORING BOOK FOR TEENS VOL 1

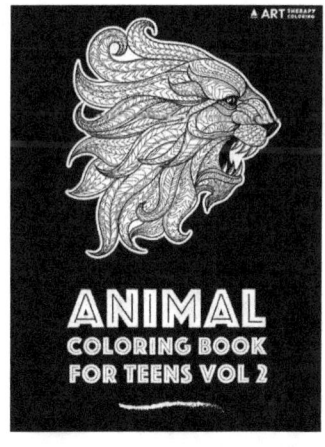

ANIMAL COLORING BOOK FOR TEENS VOL 2

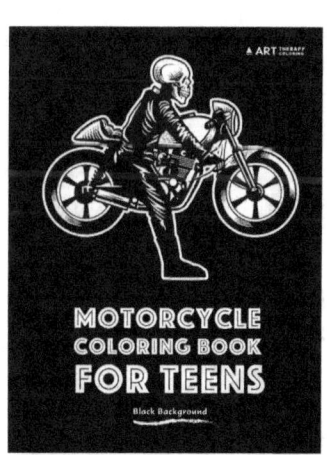

MOTORCYCLE COLORING BOOK FOR TEENS
Black Background

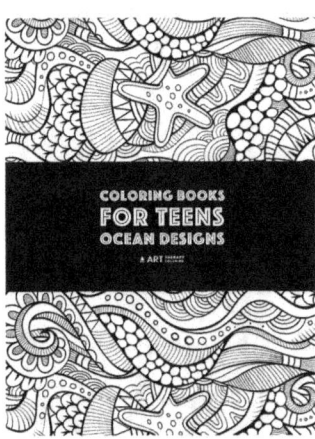

COLORING BOOKS FOR TEENS OCEAN DESIGNS

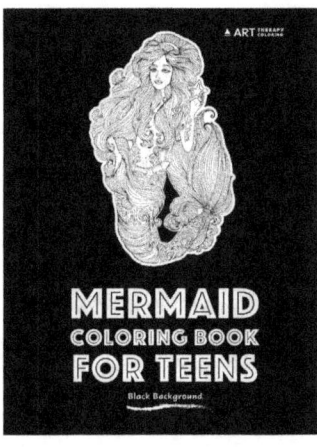

MERMAID COLORING BOOK FOR TEENS
Black Background

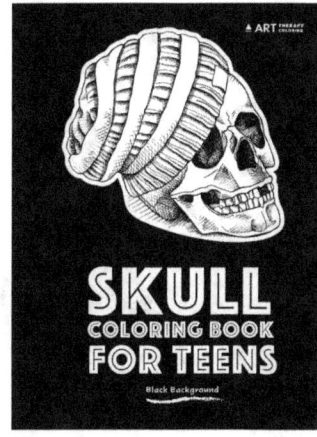

SKULL COLORING BOOK FOR TEENS
Black Background

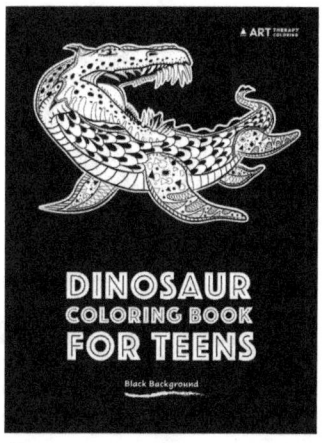

DINOSAUR COLORING BOOK FOR TEENS
Black Background

Coloring Books For Girls

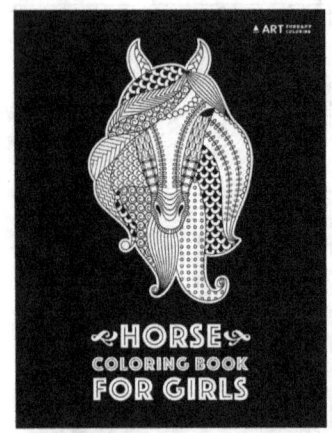

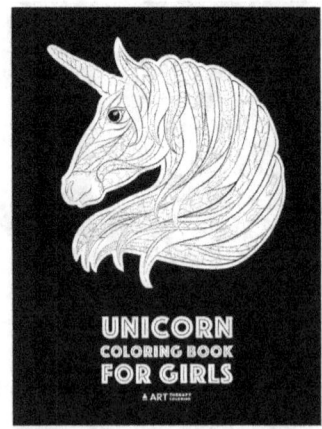

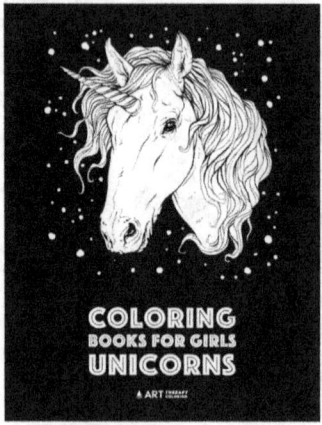

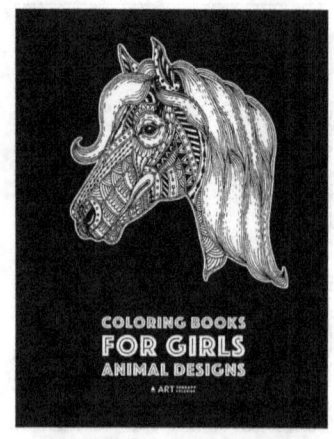

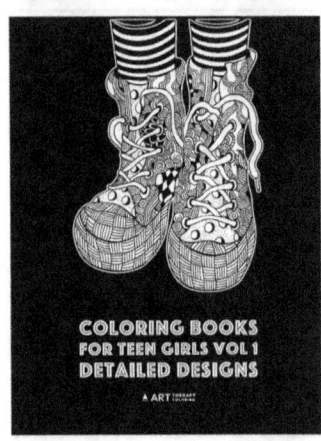

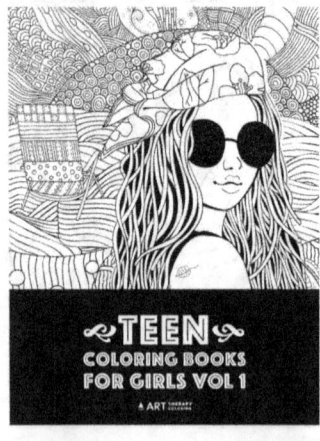

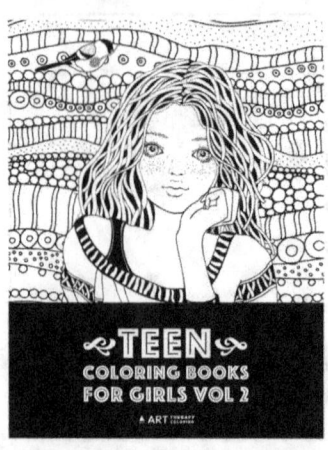

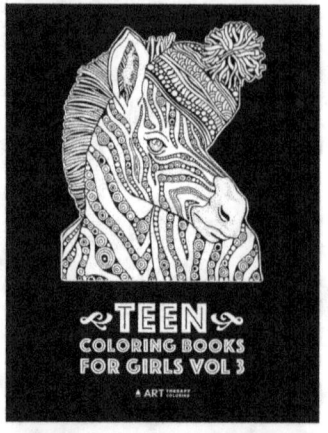

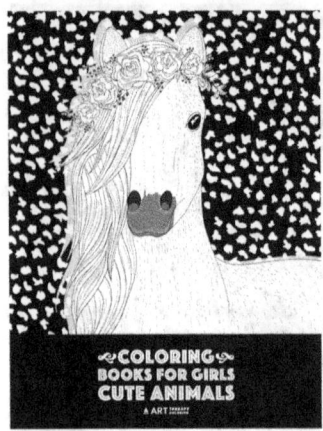

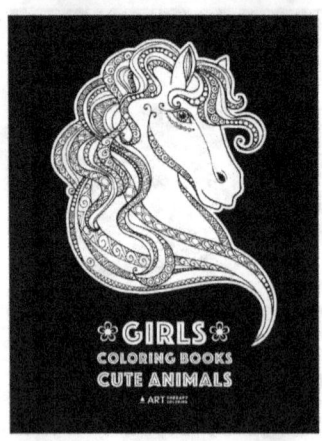

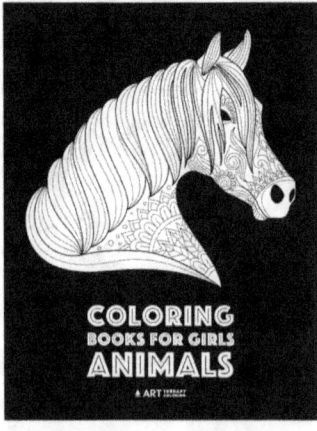

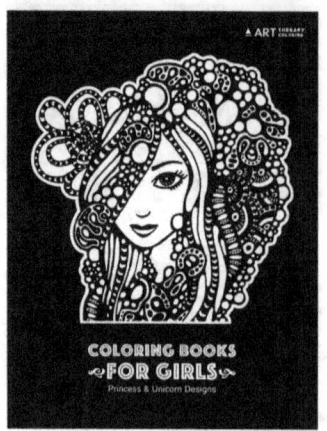

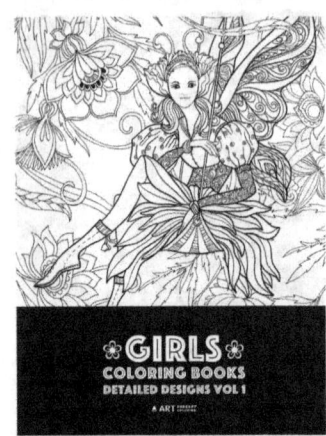

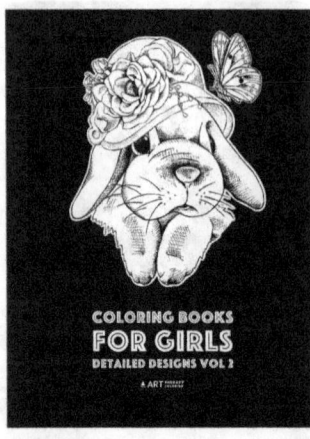

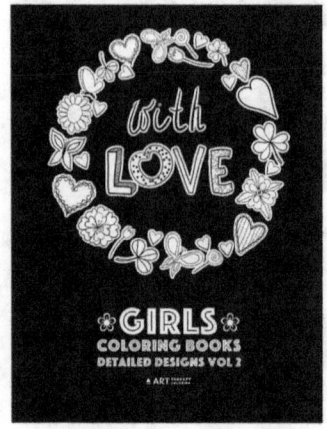

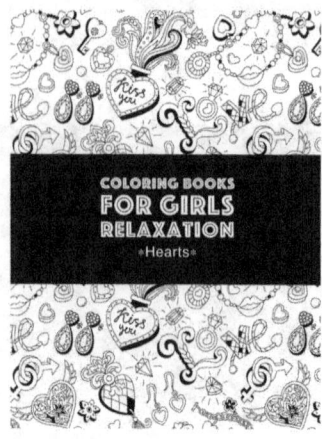

Art Therapy Coloring Books

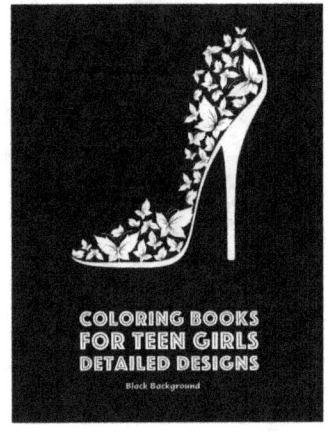

COLORING BOOKS
FOR TEEN GIRLS
DETAILED DESIGNS
Black Background

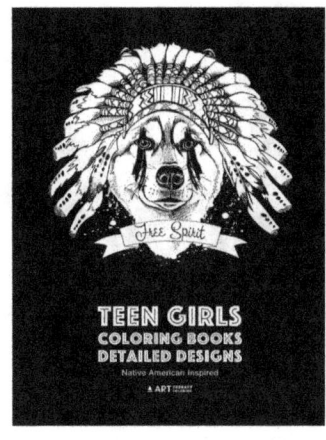

TEEN GIRLS
COLORING BOOKS
DETAILED DESIGNS
Native American Inspired

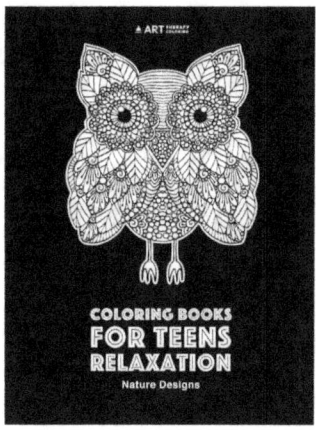

COLORING BOOKS
FOR TEENS
RELAXATION
Nature Designs

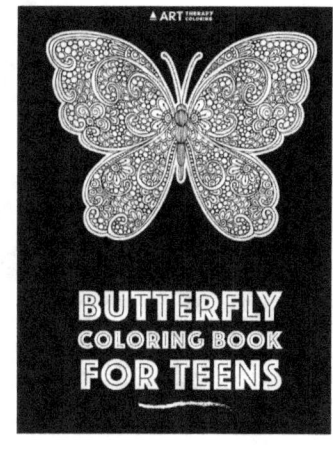

BUTTERFLY
COLORING BOOK
FOR TEENS

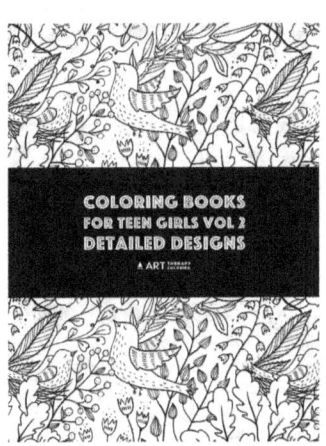

COLORING BOOKS
FOR TEEN GIRLS VOL 2
DETAILED DESIGNS

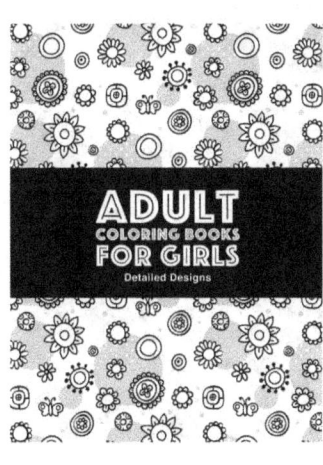

ADULT
COLORING BOOKS
FOR GIRLS
Detailed Designs

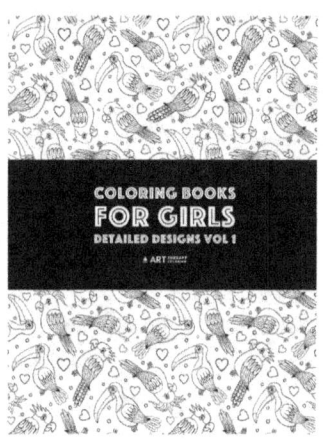

COLORING BOOKS
FOR GIRLS
DETAILED DESIGNS VOL 1

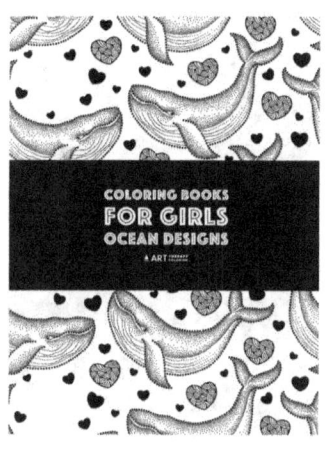

COLORING BOOKS
FOR GIRLS
OCEAN DESIGNS

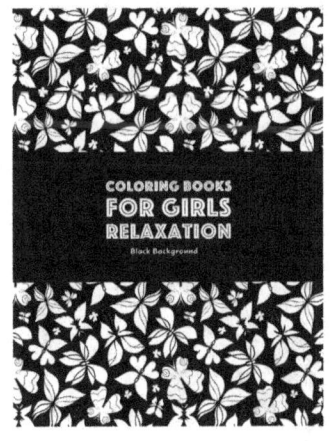

COLORING BOOKS
FOR GIRLS
RELAXATION
Black Background

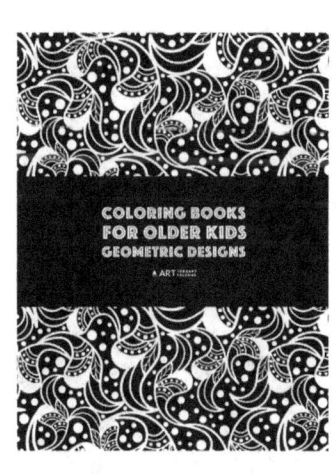

COLORING BOOKS
FOR OLDER KIDS
GEOMETRIC DESIGNS

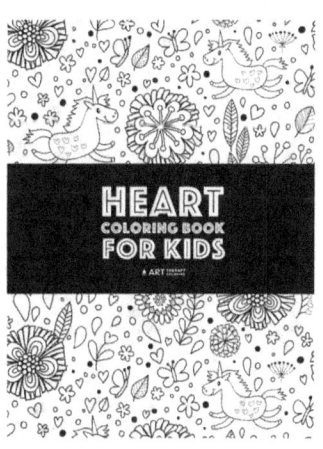

HEART
COLORING BOOK
FOR KIDS

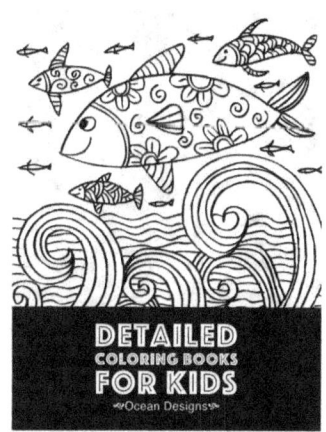

DETAILED
COLORING BOOKS
FOR KIDS
Ocean Designs

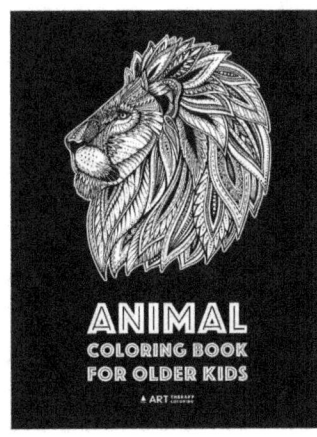

ANIMAL
COLORING BOOK
FOR OLDER KIDS

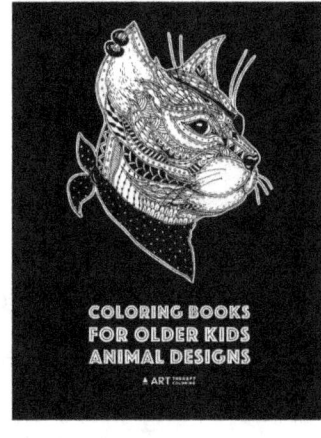

COLORING BOOKS
FOR OLDER KIDS
ANIMAL DESIGNS

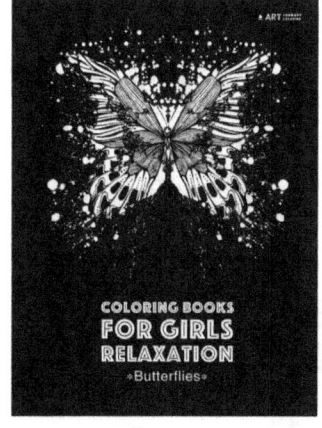

COLORING BOOKS
FOR GIRLS
RELAXATION
Butterflies

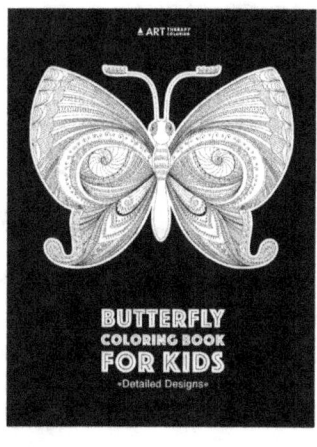

BUTTERFLY
COLORING BOOK
FOR KIDS
Detailed Designs

Coloring Books For Boys

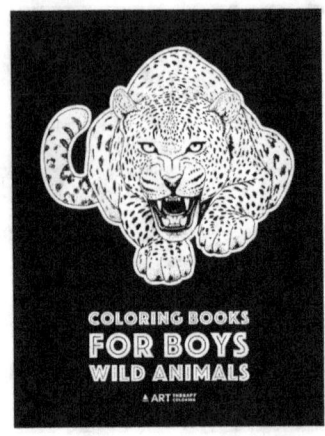

COLORING BOOKS
FOR BOYS
WILD ANIMALS
ART THERAPY COLORING

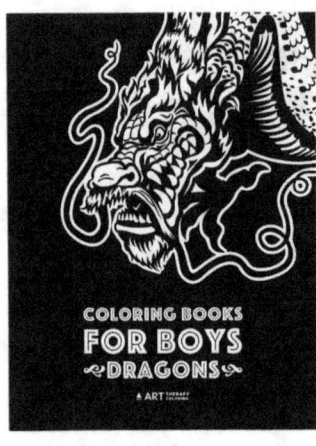

COLORING BOOKS
FOR BOYS
~DRAGONS~
ART THERAPY COLORING

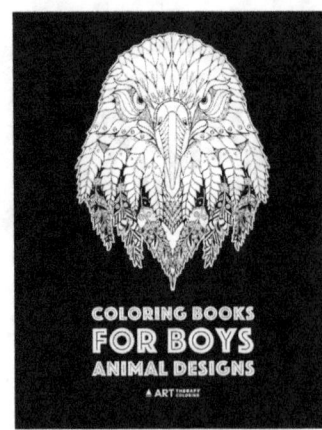

COLORING BOOKS
FOR BOYS
ANIMAL DESIGNS
ART THERAPY COLORING

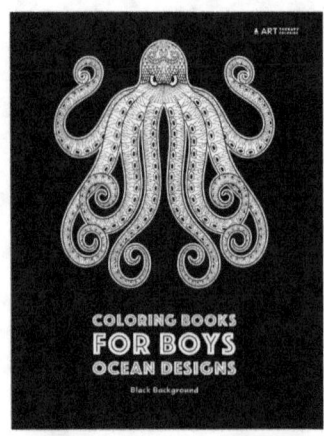

COLORING BOOKS
FOR BOYS
OCEAN DESIGNS
Black Background

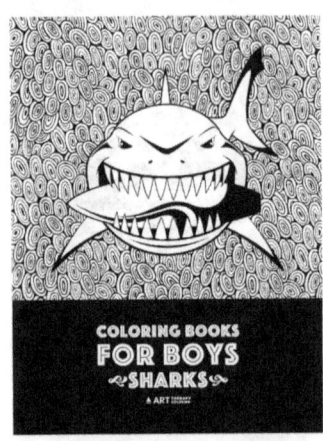

COLORING BOOKS
FOR BOYS
~SHARKS~

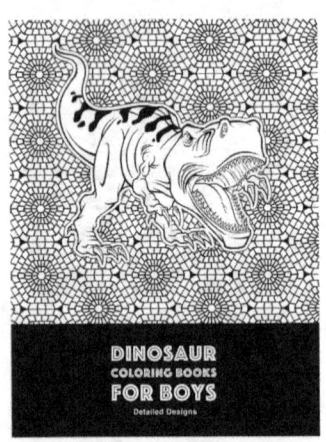

DINOSAUR
COLORING BOOKS
FOR BOYS
Detailed Designs

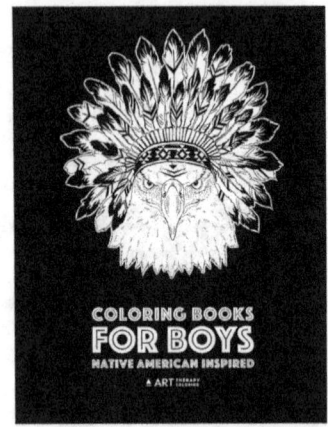

COLORING BOOKS
FOR BOYS
NATIVE AMERICAN INSPIRED
ART THERAPY COLORING

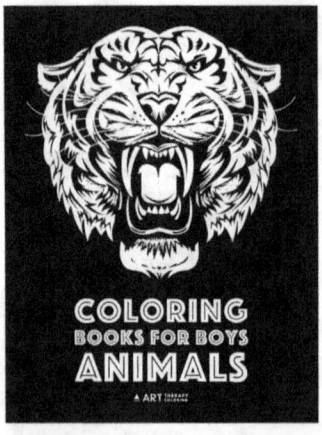

COLORING
BOOKS FOR BOYS
ANIMALS
ART THERAPY COLORING

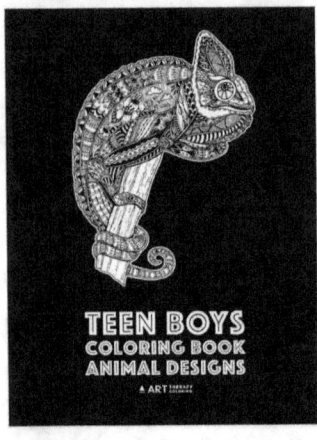

TEEN BOYS
COLORING BOOK
ANIMAL DESIGNS
ART THERAPY COLORING

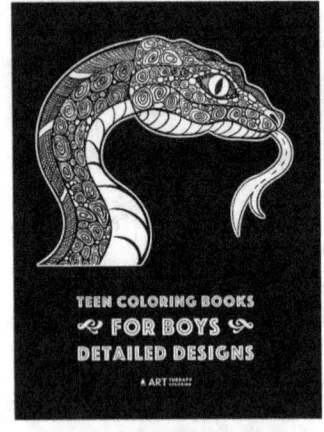

TEEN COLORING BOOKS
~ **FOR BOYS** ~
DETAILED DESIGNS
ART THERAPY COLORING

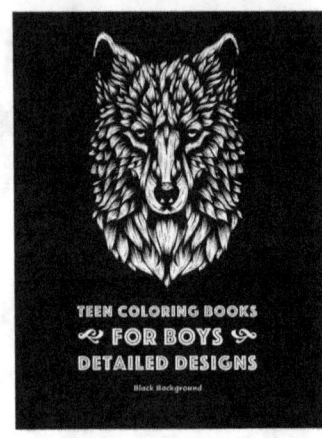

TEEN COLORING BOOKS
~ **FOR BOYS** ~
DETAILED DESIGNS
Black Background

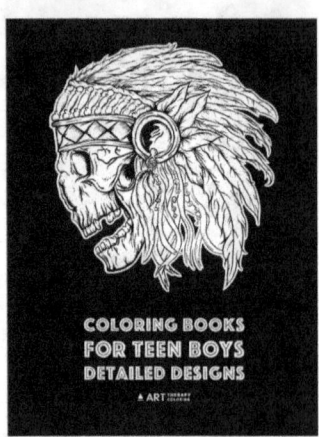

COLORING BOOKS
FOR TEEN BOYS
DETAILED DESIGNS
ART THERAPY COLORING

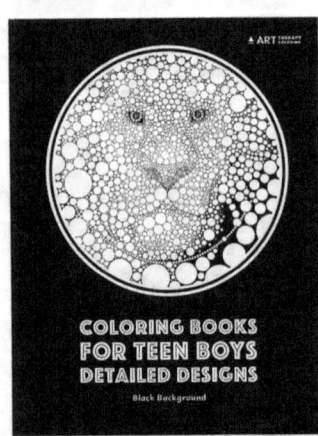

COLORING BOOKS
FOR TEEN BOYS
DETAILED DESIGNS
Black Background

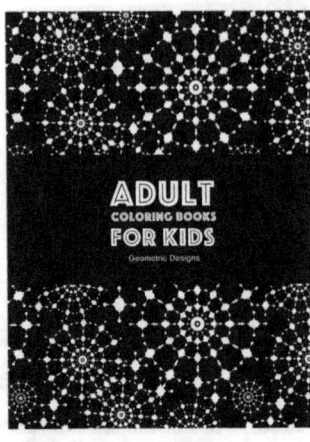

ADULT
COLORING BOOKS
FOR KIDS
Geometric Designs

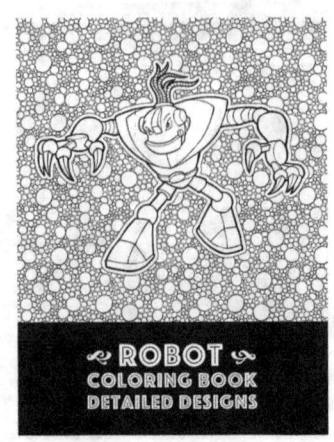

~ **ROBOT** ~
COLORING BOOK
DETAILED DESIGNS

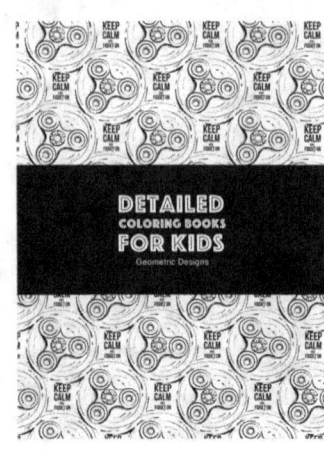

DETAILED
COLORING BOOKS
FOR KIDS
Geometric Designs

Coloring Books For Kids

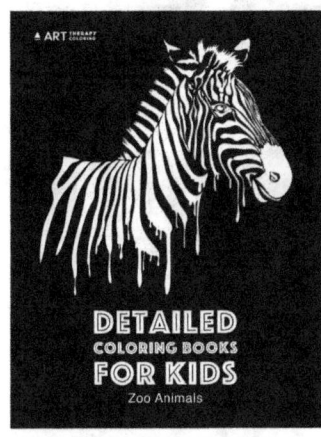

DETAILED
COLORING BOOKS
FOR KIDS
Zoo Animals

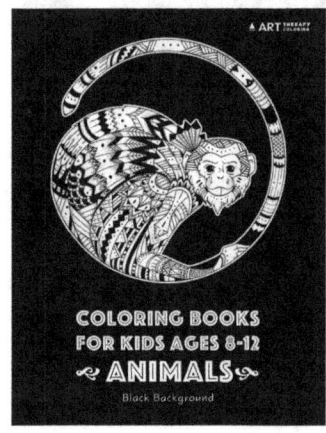

COLORING BOOKS
FOR KIDS AGES 8-12
ANIMALS
Black Background

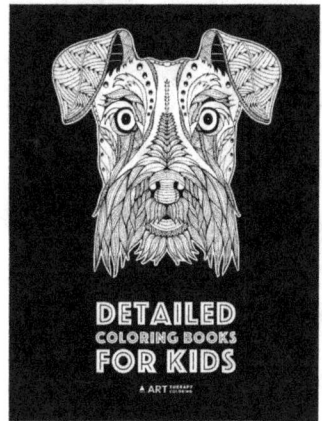

DETAILED
COLORING BOOKS
FOR KIDS

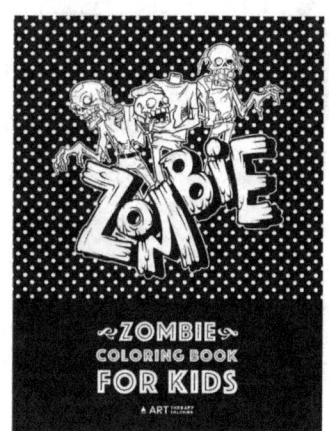

ZOMBIE
COLORING BOOK
FOR KIDS

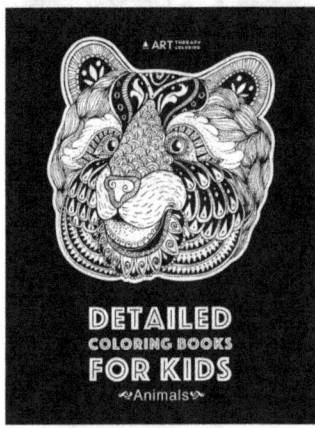

DETAILED
COLORING BOOKS
FOR KIDS
Animals

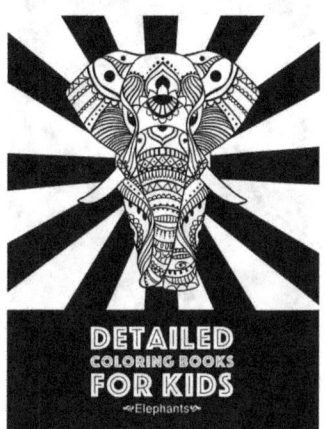

DETAILED
COLORING BOOKS
FOR KIDS
Elephants

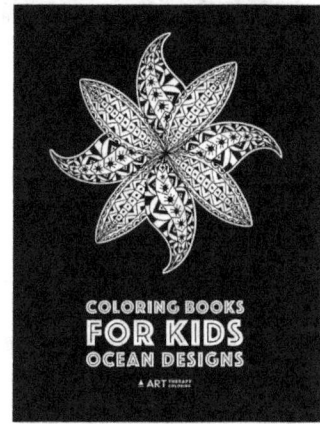

COLORING BOOKS
FOR KIDS
OCEAN DESIGNS

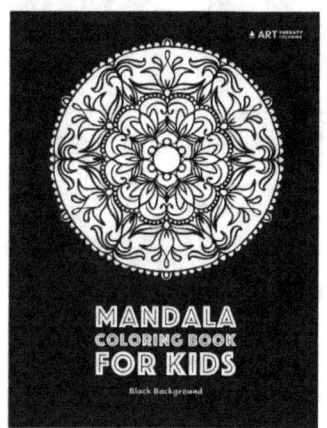

MANDALA
COLORING BOOK
FOR KIDS
Black Background

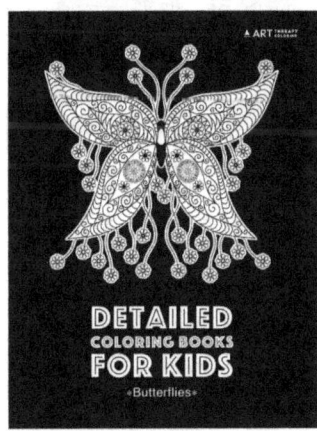

DETAILED
COLORING BOOKS
FOR KIDS
Butterflies

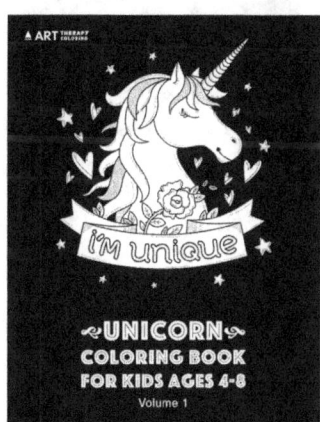

UNICORN
COLORING BOOK
FOR KIDS AGES 4-8
Volume 1

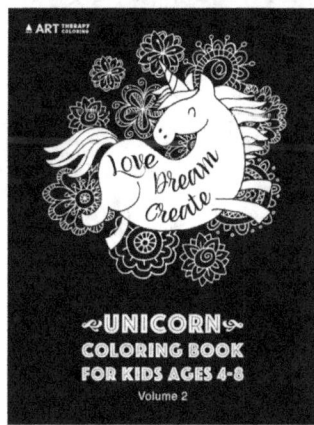

UNICORN
COLORING BOOK
FOR KIDS AGES 4-8
Volume 2

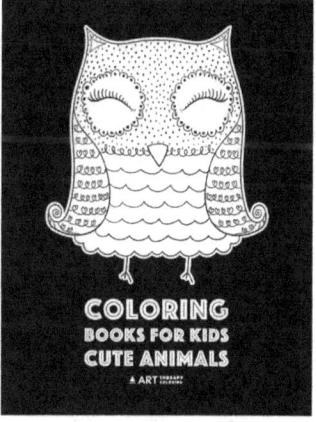

COLORING
BOOKS FOR KIDS
CUTE ANIMALS

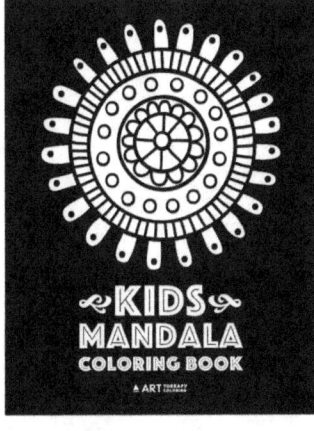

KIDS
MANDALA
COLORING BOOK

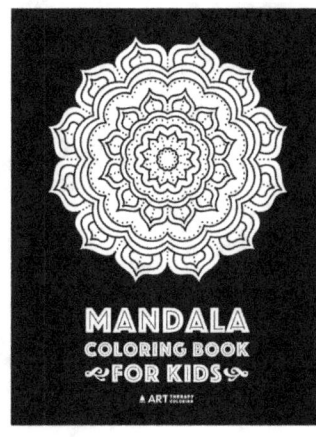

MANDALA
COLORING BOOK
FOR KIDS

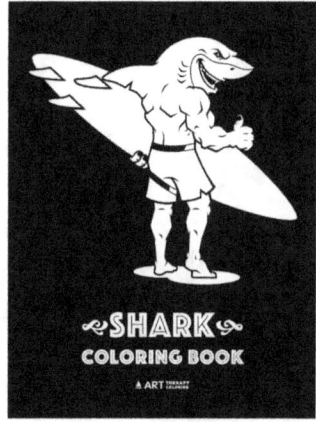

SHARK
COLORING BOOK

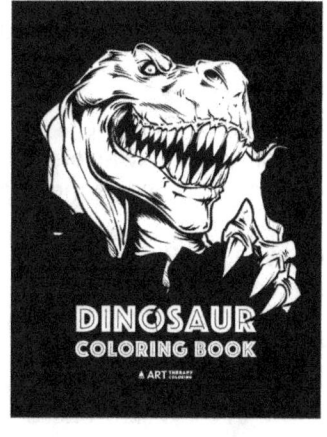

DINOSAUR
COLORING BOOK

Coloring Books For Special Occasions

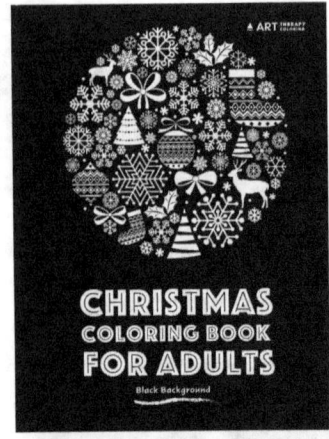
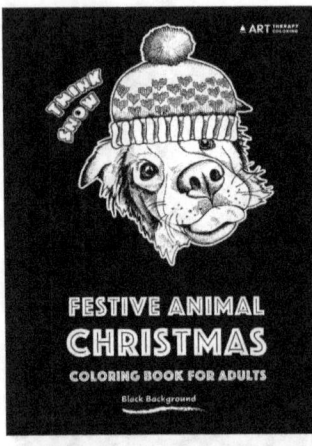
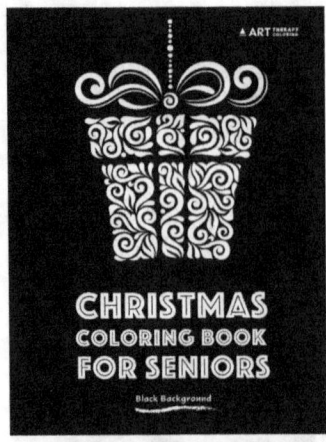
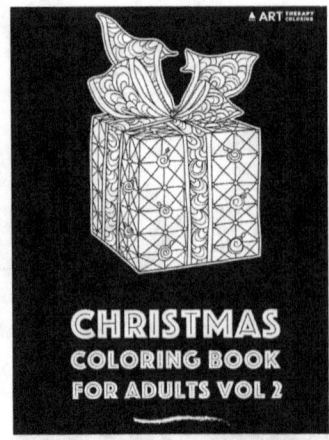

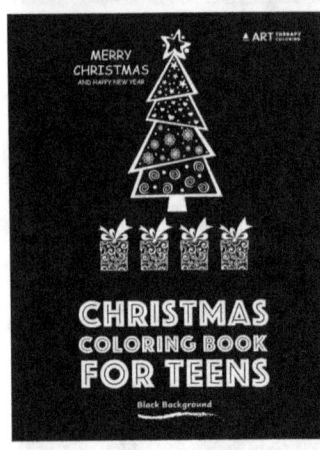
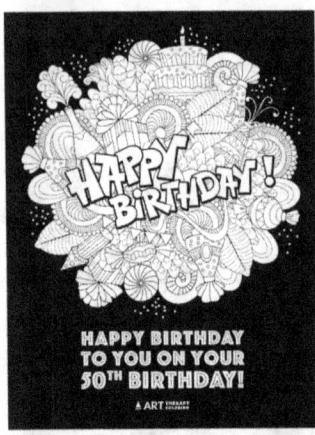
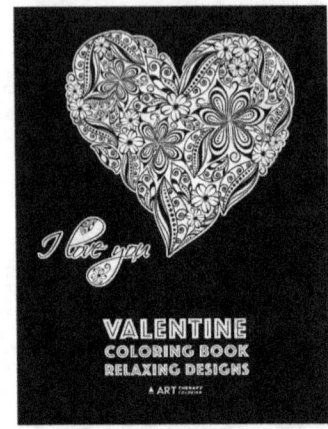
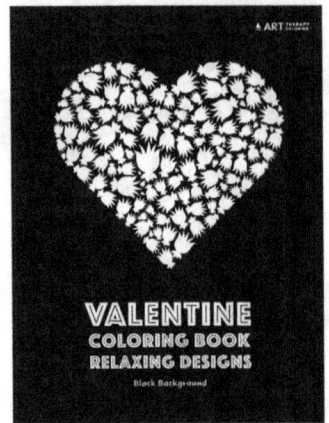

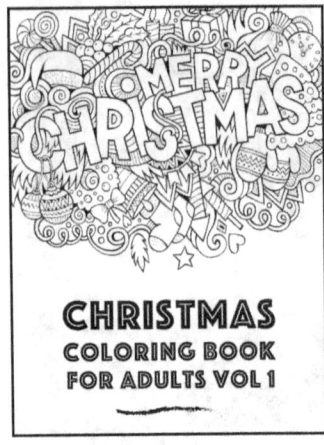
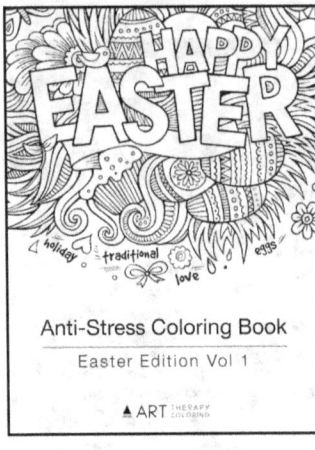
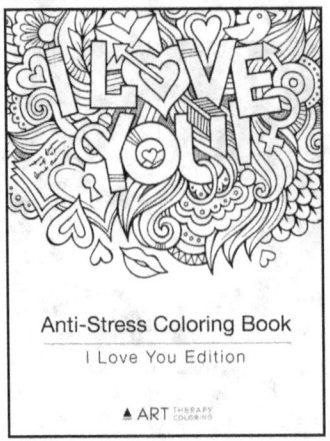
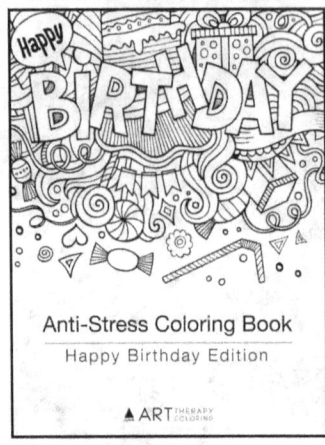

Wolf Coloring Book For Adults

Published by:
Art Therapy Coloring
El Dorado Hills, California
www.arttherapycoloring.com

Shutterstock Images

ISBN: 978-1-64126-026-8